bond that can grow between a human being and an animal in that terrifying climate. Daily work consumes every waking minute. Even as she walks from task to task, she knits socks and mittens, gathers birch twigs by moonlight. She fishes, cleaning eighty or ninety whitefish a day, skis back and forth from the farm to the fishing station morning and night to care for the beasts and people left behind. At the close of a day, her skirt, frozen, stands on the floor of the room like a barrel. Hers is a world so removed that people are dangerously carried away by their own stubborn notions (Old Johan washes his back and stomach with kerosene and dies; Young Johan sews his own wound with a needle and thread).

Anna's life is constant labor, constant watchfulness, constant giving. It is a life without rest. But Anna's openhearted and unceasing effort through the years to do the best for her people, despite the long mistrust of the farm mistress and the almost total inability of the farmer and his son to voice their gratitude, makes that life—and the story she tells—abundant in wisdom, triumph, even joy.

Dagfinn Grönoset was born in Trysil, Norway, in 1920. He is an editor of *Östlendingen,* a newspaper in the Norwegian city of Elverum. A working journalist, he is also the author of eleven books.

ANNA

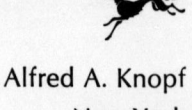

Alfred A. Knopf
New York
1975

ANNA

by Dagfinn Grönoset

Translated from the Norwegian
by Ingrid B. Josephson

With an Afterword
by Siegfried Lenz

THIS IS A BORZOI BOOK
PUBLISHED BY ALFRED A. KNOPF, INC.

Copyright © 1975 by Alfred A. Knopf, Inc.

All rights reserved under International and Pan-American Copyright Conventions. Published in the United States by Alfred A. Knopf, Inc., New York, and simultaneously in Canada by Random House of Canada Limited, Toronto. Distributed by Random House, Inc., New York. Originally published in Norway as *Anna i odemarka* by H. Aschehoug & Co., Oslo. Copyright © 1972 by H. Aschehoug & Co. (W. Nygaard). Afterword originally published in Germany, © Hoffmann und Campe Verlag, Hamburg 1973.

Library of Congress Cataloging in Publication Data
Grönoset, Dagfinn.   Anna.
Translation of Anna i odemarka.
1. Anna pa Haugsetvolden.   I.   Title.
CT1308.A67G7613   1975   301.44'93'0924[B]   74-21316
ISBN 0-394-48986-1

Manufactured in the United States of America
Published March 27, 1975
Second Printing, May 1975

A series of photographs depicting Anna's life at Haugsetvolden, taken by the author, follow pages 54 and 86.

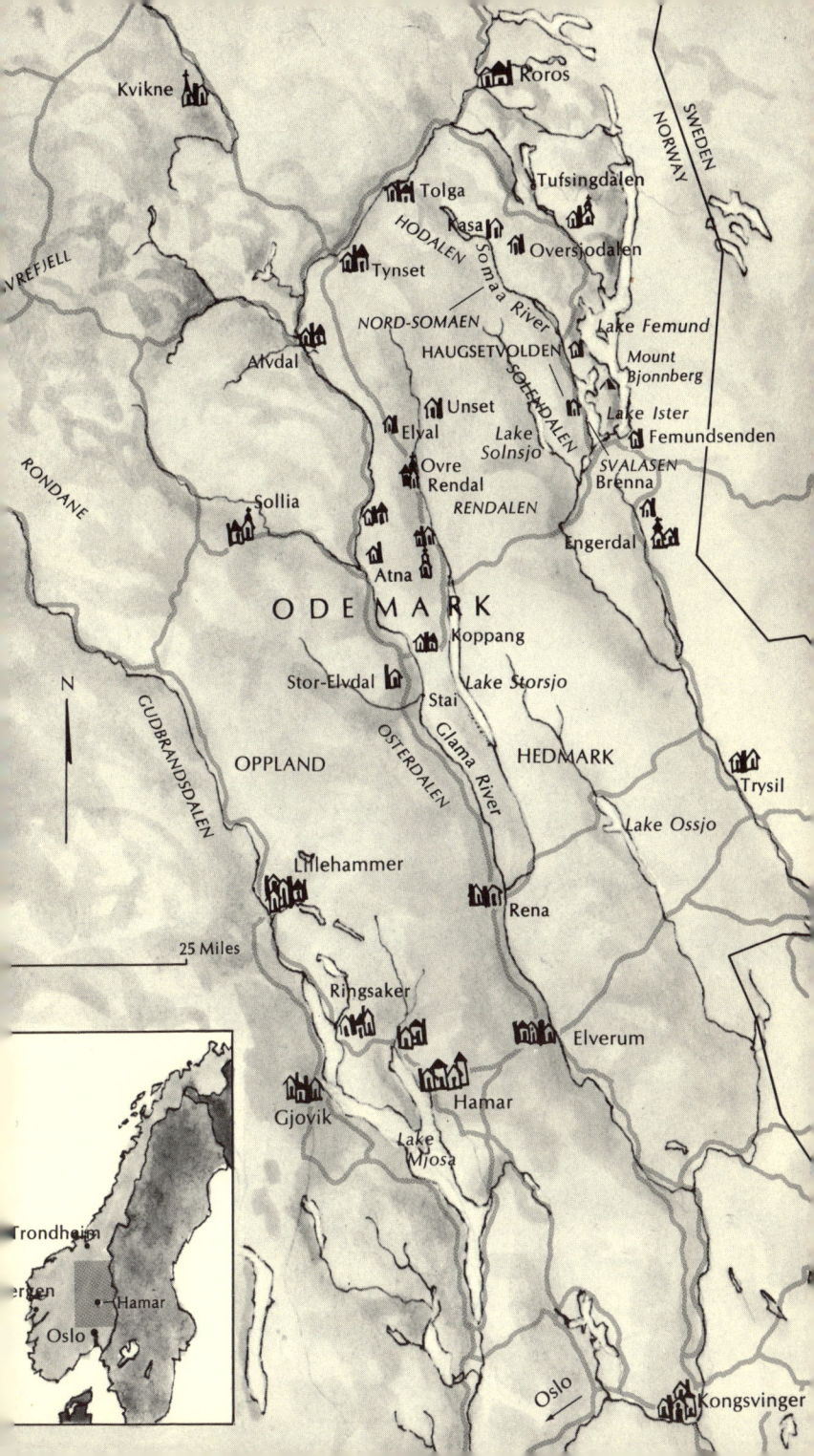

ANNA

1

"Haugsetvolden bought me. My husband sold me for three hundred kroner."

Anna hadn't meant to talk about this, ever. She didn't think it concerned anyone but herself. However, she had often noticed that people seemed to know something. So, when she was left all alone on Haugsetvolden farm and no longer had any need to show consideration for other people's feelings, she decided that she might as well speak openly. She would put all her cards on the table and describe what she knew of herself and life on Haugsetvolden.

It was on a day in April 1928 that Anna first arrived at Haugsetvolden. She came across the lake, wading through the slush on the ice, worn out by all the years of wandering along the roads of Norway, through the valleys Gudbrandsdalen and Osterdalen. She had almost no clothes to wear and had eaten little or nothing during the past few days.

There were five people living on Haugsetvolden at that time, and they needed Anna. So, when Big Karl, to whom Anna was married, said he was prepared to sell her, a deal was made. Anna has belonged to Haugsetvolden ever since and has made an incredible contribution. It was a wilderness. There were no roads around Haugsetvolden; the place was completely isolated—it was ten miles to the nearest neighbor in Glotberget. The only way she could get that far was across Lake Ister, by boat in the summertime and on skis in the winter. A trail led over the mountains to the west; it was five miles to Rendalen by way of Solendalen.

This was the trail traveled by a strange little group, coming from Rendalen to Lake Ister about 140 years ago; a woman was making the trek over the mountains with her six small children. She was fearless and strong, and her name was Gjertrud Jonsdatter Somaen. She had lost her husband in an accident in Rendalen when he fell from his horse and was killed. After that happened, she could think of no other way to survive than to move into the wilderness near Lake Ister. She and her children took over an old fishing cabin, where they lived for a long time until, through hard work, she managed to put up a log cabin and a small cow shed on Haugsetvolden.

Anna has often had Gjertrud on her mind when life at Haugsetvolden seemed hardest. She still thinks of her when the smoke rises from the weathered old cabin. It's as if Anna were still feeding the first fire lit by Gjertrud. These two women have much in common: neither one abandoned an inhuman struggle and both left their mark on the wilderness. Through the years, when Anna came up the slope with freshly caught fish for the people to whom she had given her life, she often thought of Gjertrud. Gjertrud must have felt the same way when she brought her catch home to her children. At such times, it always made Anna happy to know that Gjertrud had felt as she did: "I am needed."

This feeling has enriched Anna's life in the wilderness and given it meaning. She talks about her years on Haugsetvolden in a calm and serious way. The words are simple, the voice deep and filled with nostalgia. Hard work has taken its toll, but strength still permeates her everyday living. She quickly realized that her tasks would be many and hard, yet she never avoided them. She saw a challenge and a meaning in everything. Her only comment is: "I have laid down my life on Haugsetvolden."

Anna is eighty-two years old now and she lives all alone on her farm in the mountains. It would grieve her greatly not to be surrounded each day by what she knows so well. She often stands by the window, looking out on Lake Ister or at the Femund mountains farther east—these frame the landscape she loves. It is roomy and lonely here, wide open and quiet. Anna likes it this way. She is in touch with nature; her outlook reflects the spirit and substance of all time.

Anna often had to show the world a harder face than she might have wished. Poverty compelled her to do so. Poverty has been a part of Anna's life for as far back as she can remember. Once when she was a little girl at home on Naeroset in Ringsaker, she was playing innocently until she accidentally happened upon the country road—a great adventure in her small daily life. But she was soon met with harsh words from her mother: "Don't go running on the highway, displaying your rags, Anna!"

Living conditions were poor on the land near Lake Ister for Anna. Rags and hunger were in good supply. Only her indomitable willpower overcame a merciless existence.

The story of Anna of Haugsetvolden did not

begin in the wilderness. Her life began in Hedmark and, from the start, she met with an unkind fate.

"I was three years old when I was placed with strangers for the first time. My father brought me there. We walked along a gully with high fences on either side of it and farms all around us. I was carrying a small bundle with my christening dress inside. It was snowy white with lots of lace and ribbons. At first, I trudged behind my father, then he led me by the hand, and, finally, I got so tired that he had to carry me. The roadway was rocky and difficult.

"I think my father found it hard to leave me after he had delivered me to the farm where I was going to stay. 'I'll come back to see you, I promise,' my father said when he left. I can still hear those words, whenever I choose. They were the only consolation I had, the only good thing to think about.

"I often needed to remember what my father had said. Everything was hopeless. The farmer's wife had tuberculosis, she stayed in bed and was always vomiting. A wooden bowl with junipers in it stood by her bedside. She spat into it. If the wife brought up blood, the others in the farmhouse threw me out of doors. I would lie there until hunger took hold of me and made me come in and cry for a few crumbs.

"I was terrified of the farmer. He beat me terribly

at times. I was afraid of water and he was going to cure me of that. The worst day of all arrived when I watched him take my beautiful christening robe, which I loved so dearly, and stuff it into the stove. He burned the only precious thing I had. I cried, I screamed. The big, ugly, bearded man was cold as ice. He just slammed the stove door shut and let me scream.

"One day we were having water soup for dinner. It was made of water, rye flour, and salt. I happened to spill some that day, a few drops fell on the floor. Anger took hold of him again, until I thought he was the devil himself. He made me lick the soup off the floor. I was down on all fours, like a cat, licking up what it had been my misfortune to spill. I can still feel the rough and splintery floorboards on my tongue—it was like licking sandpaper. Everything tasted bad but I didn't dare spit anything out. I had been scared to death ever since the farmer burned my christening dress.

"I stayed on the farm till the fall. My grandmother came to fetch me then. The following winter I was allowed to stay home, but the next summer I was sent away again. This time I went somewhere else, but I was afraid it would be just as bad a place as the last. When my grandmother, who had brought me, was ready to leave, I was mad with fear. I ran after her, I desperately wanted to go back home. I didn't yet understand that poverty is hard and pitiless.

"On this farm, they had taken in a pauper woman —her name was Agnethe. I thought she was ugly and awful and was out to get me. She lay in bed, sniffing dry tobacco up her nose. The people on the farm wanted me to sleep in the same bed with her. I would sit next to her in the dark and wait for her to fall asleep. She smelled of tobacco and piss. As soon as I heard her breathing heavily, gurgling in her throat, I would sneak out of bed and curl up in a corner in the main room. I would sit there in fear, until I managed to fall asleep.

"One day, the people on the farm found me in the corner of the main room. They understood how much I hated sharing a bed with the old woman and I got a bed to myself. They were nice to me on that farm, only the beggar woman scared me. She had such piercing, strange eyes—eyes that made you think she was ready to scream. It also seemed very strange to me that she lay in bed with a pipe in her mouth. The pillow was covered with brown tobacco stains.

"That fall Grandmother came to pick me up. I was unhappy again. I wanted to stay and hid behind some currant bushes in the garden. That's where I was standing, crying, when they found me. Grandmother was a hard woman and I felt she had never been crueler than on that day. She grabbed my arm so roughly that it hurt, and we hurried toward home without exchanging a word. I dreaded everything.

"I never felt that I had a home. I certainly didn't know what security was—hardly knew what happiness was either. If I was happy, I didn't dare show it. I loved flowers and felt like singing when I found an anemone by the outside wall, but I kept everything inside me. I was uncertain and confused. I experienced things I wanted to talk about and ask about, but I didn't dare to and said nothing. I shut everything in.

"Neither did I learn to understand things when I was old enough to go to school. There were not many weeks of school and I didn't go to half of them. My mother refused to let me go; she needed me for the daily work. In the summer, I ran after her to the outfarm, to Lorta. That is where I got my first training in hard work. Mother woke me up at five each morning. Sometimes, I would fall back in bed, dazed and exhausted. It was no use begging for mercy; out and to work! was the order. For me, that meant carrying water, milking the cows, and cleaning the cow shed. I often felt that my mother was very strict. Later on, I understood that she had to be. She was a dairymaid for other people, a servant who was not permitted to make her own decisions, and she was marked by that. There was something restless, fearful, and distressed about her; she had an unsureness that always made me feel unsafe. I preferred hiding in a corner to sitting on her lap. Since then I have thought that she was rarely calm because she somehow feared the people she worked for.

"Even so, I remember life on the Lorta outfarm with pleasure, in spite of the hard days. The outfarm was in a lonely, wooded mountain area, far from other people and their rural life. In some ways I felt like a bird of ill omen, having been placed with strangers at the age of three, where everyone was cold to me and wanted to hurt me. I held on to my shirt and my slice of bread more tightly than the other kids."

"At the age of eight, I fought my way to school. We were on the outfarm at the time and my mother needed me there. However, I wanted to go to school so badly that I didn't hesitate to threaten her: 'If you don't let me go to school, I will report you, the whole village will know that you refuse to let me go!' My poor mother could neither read nor write herself. She wasn't stupid, just a neglected human being. So I was allowed to go to school with my sister Sina.

"School turned out to be something special for me; for the first time in my life, I had something to hold on to. It went well from the start; I was sure that this suited something inside me. One day, I was told that I would be the class monitor. I thrived on that. Soon afterward, I was also put to teaching the youngest children. That gave me an indescribable feeling. For the first time I had confidence in myself and knew that someone needed me. Among the youngest children was a 'backward' boy, who didn't understand much of what went on in the schoolroom. I took a special interest in that boy and sat with him for hours, day after day. Every time things went well, if he grasped and understood a letter or a word, we were both happy. I think I was probably the happier one. I was experiencing something new, I was helping another human being. It made such a big impression on me that I wanted to help some more. That's why I skipped eagerly along the road from Lorta every school day. The strange thing was that from then on, it was much easier to help my mother. I was able to do so much, I wanted to do so much. I no longer kept everything inside myself; I even started singing a little.

"The last day of exams turned out to be a black day. It was May 16, a lovely spring day—the leaves had opened and the entire village of Ringsaker smelled of fields being burned for new planting. It was a day made for feeling happy and—dressing up. I cried that day. I didn't have the clothes that other people did. My mother came to me with a simple, plaid, homespun dress my sister had worn. The dress was so old that my elbows stuck out through large holes and it hung around me in rags. 'You *will* wear that dress,' she commanded. She also brought me an old slip to wear under it. That was the worst thing of all, but there was nothing to be done. I went to exam-day with rags flapping. I met the other schoolgirls—so clean, so happy in their new, bright colors. I thought I had never seen anything so pretty. I wished with all my heart that my dress had at least been mended. It wouldn't have been so bad then, the rags wouldn't have shown.

"One of the women in the neighborhood dropped by on exam-day and saw my dress. She understood that I was wretched. She suddenly said: 'Anna, you can move in with me and work for your confirmation clothes. You will wear a pretty dress . . .' I didn't have to think it over. I went to the woman's neighboring farm the same day, in the ragged dress I had worn to exams. I didn't bring so much as a small bundle. However, on the day I was confirmed in the chapel in Asmarka that fall, I was dressed just as prettily as the other girls.

"It was a wonderful day."

2

After her confirmation, Anna worked on several farms in Ringsaker. She was used to working hard and didn't give it much thought. She did miss being in touch, however; she had no girl friends and the only thing that added some cheer to her life was a dance now and then—in the summer in a barn and in the winter in somebody's house. Anna was light-footed and loved to dance; she was never a wallflower. Everybody wanted to dance with Anna.

In the summer of 1918 a stranger came to Ringsaker. He was Big Karl, a large, strong, handsome man. He had come across the border from Sweden, where he was born, and was working as a lumberjack in Asmarka. He was restless and uneasy, a vagabond who only worked occasionally and had no permanent place to live. However, in the tiny rural society where Anna lived, Big Karl was something new and exciting. He was one of the free spirits of the road, and for Anna he was adventure itself. When Big Karl showed up at the barn dance one Saturday night, waltzing, wild, and warm, Anna fell in love for the first time. The barn dance in Asmarka was the beginning of a life that would be anything but easy. Anna longed for a home. She felt she had never had one and thought her dream might come true with Big Karl.

Two years after the barn dance the wedding bells were ringing in the whitewashed church at Mjosstranda in Ringsaker. Anna and Big Karl were married.

"On Whitsunday, June 5, 1921, I left Ringsaker for good. I turned my back on my home town; I was scared, but full of excitement. Big Karl and I carried almost nothing except the few brooms he had made out of horsehair. We sold them to the farmers on our way. We walked through the valley Gudbrandsdalen, sleeping in haystacks and empty barns, under thick branches or the open sky. We had practically no money or food. I often went hungry. Even then, I had begun to wonder what kind of a person Big Karl really was. I realized more and more that he was not the person I had believed him to be. I felt cheated and disappointed, but I was determined to keep on trying; I wasn't going to give up, no matter what. It didn't occur to me to just turn around and go back to Asmarka once I'd taken to the open road and freedom. Yet, I already sensed that to live this way was not right for me.

"Walking along the roads was so hard on my legs that by early summer, up on Mount Dovre, I had developed ugly sores. Big Karl did nothing to help. No matter how tired, downcast, and exhausted I became, he did nothing to cheer me up. I was merely told to go on."

In September, the same year Anna and Big Karl had left Ringsaker, they finally reached the region of open fields called Femundsmarka in the valley Oversjodalen in Nord-Osterdal. They were utterly destitute by that time, but Anna was going to work for Jacob Rostbakken Oyen to earn something to eat.

After a few days, however, Big Karl wanted to move on—the restless bird had to feel air beneath his wings.

"We went to the valley Hodalen, to Elias Tangen's place. The people there realized my plight and asked me if I didn't want to stay. Big Karl wanted to leave, but we had to have food, so I earned the bread for both of us.

"Big Karl got worse and worse, most of the time he was out getting drunk with a Swede who lived nearby. He became more and more demanding and inconsiderate as time went by. His restlessness and uneasiness increased as well, so we had to try and move on once again. We walked from farm to farm, I worked here and there while Big Karl went off on expeditions selling his horsehair brooms for weeks on end. He'd come back, broke and hungry, and take every penny I'd earned. He never had any to spare for me. But at least I got to eat on the farms where I worked.

"One day in the early spring, Big Karl and I came trudging through Sollia—we had no money and no food. But Knut Eggen had bought twenty-five acres of land, which he planned to plow and clear of rocks. The rocks were to be piled into fences—hard and senseless work for a woman—but I took on the job. I started piling up rocks while snow was still on the ground, and I labored all through the summer. My back and my hands gave me a lot of trouble. My hands were numb and hurt all night long, as if they were burning up. Many times I thought my situation was hopeless. I worked out of hunger, but I behaved as if I were the one who had bought the land. I was determined to do the job. I *would finish* it, no matter what. If I didn't do the work as it should be done, no one would believe in me. In that case, I would be a failure. To me that meant I would never get anywhere. I would have lost the last remnant of self-respect."

"Big Karl and I roamed about for two years before we returned once again to Oyen in Oversjodalen. Time after time I tried to stop him, asked him to pull himself together, to realize that we couldn't go on living this way. Jacob Oyen often told me that the time had come for me to turn my back on Big Karl and to let him move on by himself. Jacob could see the kind of crazy fellow Big Karl was—that he had no backbone whatever. Jacob also understood how much it cost me to stay with Big Karl. Still, I wanted to stay. I suffered defeat after defeat. I tried to talk sense into him, but, what with the aimless, loose life he led, it was impossible to get him to change.

"So off we went again. It was wintertime and we went north toward Trondheim. One desperately cold night we stayed at an inn in Storen. It was a complete pigsty, full of the strangest people. Gypsies, vagrants, small-time crooks—none of them had a home or steady income, all living from hand to mouth. It was dangerous company for Big Karl.

There was a lot of drinking and carrying on, and it got on my nerves. I became more and more depressed.

"I often went out wandering by myself. In many ways I felt it was better for me. Often I just walked in on people and sat down. I thought: 'There must be someone who'll see who I really am and who'll understand my distress, someone who'll be willing and able to help.' Most of the time I was given food. I could never bring myself to beg, I was ashamed enough as it was.

"Once in a while it was more difficult to find a place to sleep than a place to eat. On one farm in Gudbrandsdalen, I didn't know what to do. I explained to the farmer's wife how things were with me, I even told her about Big Karl—that seemed to help a little. 'You are *begging* to stay here then?' the woman finally asked. She was doubtful and looked at me very carefully. I admitted as much. The woman didn't want to refuse me shelter and told me to go to the maids' quarters and stay there overnight. The maids, on the other hand, didn't want to put up a crow like me. 'You'll have to come this way then,' said the wife, somewhat irritated, as she took me into the stables. There she pointed to a manger in front of some horses, filled with some raw, cold hay. I buried myself in the hay. I wasn't wearing much and I thought I'd die of cold. That night I asked myself: 'Are you still a human being, Anna? Have you sunk so low that you belong with the animals?' I found no answer, I only knew that I had no choice. The next morning I went on, wretched and freezing."

"I was soon to find out that there were things in this world worse than a stable full of horses. The night before Easter, that winter, I walked into a place near Sel in Gudbrandsdalen. I had been trudging the roads for weeks; I huddled against the cold at night, meeting up with many others who were as frozen and as barely human as I. Such was the man I encountered near Sel, when I crossed his doorstep in misery, asking for a place to spend the night. He simply said no. Whatever was going to happen to me would have to happen.

"That night I walked for a long time along the country road. I was shivering all over. The stars were shining above me, cold and clear. Trees and stumps cracked noisily in the frost. I noticed an outhouse by the side of the road. It was unlocked. I didn't have the courage to walk into the farmhouse close by—I wasn't up to another 'No.' I just went into the outhouse in a kind of daze and lay down on some pressed hay I found there. I had nothing to cover myself with, and the clothes I was wearing could not keep me warm. I hadn't eaten all day and had no food whatsoever with me. On nights like that one's thoughts stand still. I was glad of it because, otherwise, desperation would have taken over. Next morning the bitter cold woke me early, feeling strange and remote. My face felt stiff and had probably turned blue. Something inside me seemed to be forcing me to move on, saying, 'Go, Anna, go . . .'

"I walked a few hundred yards. I was standing near the gate to the farm. I took a chance and walked in.

"It was the morning of Easter Sunday and only the farmer's wife was awake. I could tell from the look in her eyes that she was a little scared but that she also felt sorry for me. I told her I had slept on the hay in her outhouse. For the first time in a long while I sensed compassion—the woman clearly thought my situation pitiful. There was food on the table and she let me eat as much as I wanted. My body felt warm again and I was full of food and good cheer when I said thank you and left.

"But that bundle of hay remained on my mind and I saw it in my mind's eye whenever night fell. Strange as it may seem, I can still see it now, as if it were a ghost. Whenever I hear of people in misery, going through bad times, I think of the bundle of hay in the outhouse.

"When summer came, I got the urge to see Ringsaker again. I had been gone a long time and had no idea how I would be received in my home town.

After all, I had taken to the road with Big Karl. I also wanted to see if I could remember my childhood.

"I never got to Ringsaker; instead something happened that I'll always remember. I was walking on the road in Ringebu, feeling happier than I had in a long time. I was able to enjoy little things like flowers on the edge of a ditch or birds flying over a fence. The smells were nice and summery, like something with honey in it; everything was more open and free—once again I was feeling the way I did when I'd had the urge to sing for the first time.

"All of a sudden, I heard someone calling me. A small woman was standing on a stone fence in front of a poor cottage. I could tell right away that she was upset. She begged and pleaded with me to come inside with her. There I got the story: Her husband had run off with another woman. She didn't know where he was and was left with seven children, the youngest only three months old, the oldest not yet confirmed. What was she going to do? 'Here is a mission for you, Anna,' I thought to myself. So when the woman asked if I would stay with her and mind the children while she went out to beg, there was no doubt in my mind. In a way, she and I had a lot in common; we were both in great trouble, and besides, I liked to feel that someone needed me.

"Seven weeks went by. We managed somehow

and didn't lose our courage. Some days, the woman brought home little or nothing, other days there was enough for all of us. I noticed that the children were growing more and more fond of me; they knew someone was taking care of them, and they trusted me. Life in the tiny cottage alternated between tears and laughter, each day full and rewarding.

"Then something happened that I had never expected. One day the woman did not return. She had run away with a stranger to Sweden and I haven't seen her since. Here I was in the cottage with seven children, there was no food and no one to help us. It was an enormous responsibility, greater than I could possibly have the strength to handle. I could have gone to the authorities, but I was afraid that what I would get from them would be too little to live on for the children and myself, so I didn't dare do that. But I didn't want to give up either, I wasn't going to desert the children, so I decided to place them with people who I thought would be kind to them.

"I found out that a woman in the village wanted the youngest. He was a boy. He was my favorite. I was fondest of him because he needed the most care. The day I went out to deliver him, I kept sitting down by the side of the road. I sat looking at the boy for a long time and thought it was unfair that

I should have to give him away. It hurt, but I pulled myself together and went on.

"When I got to the farm, the woman was in the cow shed. She came running to the kitchen to take possession of him. I didn't like the woman, she didn't look kind, and she grabbed the boy's arm really hard right away, sort of yanking him toward her. The boy started screaming and wouldn't stop.

"This was more than I could stand. I was sure I was right. I just said no to the woman, took the little boy with me, and went back to our shack. The child went to sleep in my lap that night and I knew I had not done the wrong thing.

"A few days later I did find a place for the boy. I think he ended up with good people. The woman on this farm was understanding toward me as well —out of consideration for me, she quietly disappeared with the little boy into another room. That's when I took to my heels. The last thing I heard as I ran through the courtyard was the boy— he was crying.

"The only thing that kept me going was my concern for the other children. They needed me and I felt that the best I could do for them was to find people who would care for them properly. I found good people. One after the other, I delivered the children. Else and Morten went to the same farm.

Each time the same thing happened—the kids held on to my skirt and wouldn't let go.

"The day I handed over the last child, I hurried outside and almost ran along the road. I wasn't myself, the world was a mess, empty and unpleasant. I felt uncertain and needed someone to talk to. Yet when I suddenly heard a woman on the road calling my name, it sounded as if it came from far away, through a fog. I got scared and ran to the empty cottage as if my life were in danger.

"I sat in the cottage, not knowing what to do next. I had to find something to do so that I would forget the children, who I felt still needed me. I also had to earn some money. I didn't get one penny from the village for the months I had been a mother to those orphans. I was in bad shape and had to try to get away. I could probably find the kind of hard labor I was used to. The next day I would shut the door to the cottage and be on my way. . . ."

But that's not what happened. Just as she was gathering her few possessions into a bundle, Big Karl showed up. Anna felt trapped—Big Karl seemed quite remote after the hectic months with the children. She could tell at once that he had been through hard times—his face looked paler and thinner than before, his clothes were dirty and ragged.

Anna also noticed immediately that his nerves were on edge. He was full of the restlessness she knew so well, and she realized that he had come to drag her off on his wanderings again.

"I didn't have the strength to go against him, even though I knew I was getting into the same miserable existence. I could see more and more clearly that I was not suited for the vagrant's life. Every hour was torture. I had to get away, away from the road and Big Karl, or else I would go under completely. But I could see no way out.

"We walked through Folldal, Alvdal, Tynset, and Tolga, all the way to Kasa, a miserable little hamlet between the valleys Oversjodalen and Hodalen. Here I did man's work for a while until one day a man coming through Kasa told me that Jacob Oyen might consider hiring me. His only concern was that my migrant life might have ruined me and that I would soon want to take to the road again. He had said: 'I'm sure Anna won't stick it out.'

"This was a challenge. I said good-bye to Kasa and went to Jacob Oyen. I promised him that I would stay for a long time, and I stayed two years. All that time, Big Karl roamed about as usual, showing up constantly, demanding that I give him the money I had set aside and talking about how we had to move on again. I wasn't strong enough and gave in. The people on Oyen had been kind and friendly toward me, I was treated like a human being there. I soon found out what it meant to feel the opposite."

"A little later, on May 17, Big Karl and I were on our way from Elga, on the east side of Lake Femund. We intended to cross the lake and go to Gammelhytta, an old cottage on the west side, but people had warned us against it. The ice was not safe; to cross the lake was challenging fate. Big Karl refused to accept this verdict. By the way, he had a sleigh to hold on to—he gave me a hatchet. I was supposed to use it to knock on the ice and make my way as best I could.

"Big Karl raced ahead of me with his sleigh across Lake Femund in the direction of Gammelhytta. As I got closer to the west side of the lake, the ice became thinner and thinner. I knew very well that Big Karl had taken me on a perilous journey. I kept testing the ice in front of me with the hatchet and finally it was so thin that I could break it with nothing but the handle. I saw death ahead of me and expected the ice to collapse any moment. I was sure I would remain in Lake Femund that day. I prayed to God to help me or to receive me into heaven. Big Karl stood a little way from shore, cold and indifferent, watching to see how I was faring. He gave no sign that he wanted to help.

"Not far from land, a large rock stuck out. It

could save me. I wriggled forward on the ice till it rocked, and at the very moment it burst under me, I used what strength I had left to throw myself toward the stone, a plunge between life and death. Miraculously, I was able to get a grip on it and pull myself out of the icy water. I didn't dare rest in case I went stiff, so I gave another leap toward land—and got to solid ground. I was safe—and I didn't forget to thank the Lord.

"No sooner did I stand upright on the beach at the edge of Lake Femund than Big Karl got up the courage to cover the remaining distance also—quickly and confidently. With his sleigh, he reached land with no trouble at all.

"From Gammelhytta to the northern end of the lake there was no road. It was completely impassable —big, slippery, icy rocks, one after the other, blocked the way. I fell and stood up, fell again and stood up again until I could taste blood.

"I often wondered why I didn't have the courage to leave Big Karl. Many people asked me the same thing. My only answer was that I had been used to being mistreated since the time when I was growing up. I didn't know what self-assurance was and had never dared to oppose anyone. I always did what I was told and what I thought people expected of me. I never had my own way or what I wanted. I was accustomed to obeying others. Deep down inside me the truth was very different from what Big Karl could accept. Time and time again I told him he should go on alone, that I wanted to be free and could see no sense in marching along country roads, in going hungry, living without shelter, freezing in some ruin.

"Big Karl always believed I had fallen in love with somebody else, that something was going on between me and another man he didn't know about. If that turned out to be true and Big Karl found out who the other guy was, he would get a hold of him and put an end to the affair. I knew Big Karl wasn't joking—jealousy was so much a part of him that he could do the most terrible things. He told me this in no uncertain terms. His threats were hanging over me constantly and they made me very fearful. I didn't dare talk to a man because I was afraid Big Karl might hear about it. I was in no doubt as to what would happen then."

On May 1, 1926, Anna and Big Karl started out on a daring journey through the Osterdal mountains. The usual thing had happened: Anna had worked in Oversjodalen and saved up a few kroner; then Big Karl took the money and made her leave. It was a cold night and no later than four in the morning when Big Karl and Anna took to the mountains, walking in the direction of Glofoken. What little they owned they had wrapped in a small bundle and tied to their sleigh. Conditions underfoot were perfect. They were planning on going to Rendalen first.

"We got no farther than the Storlegda outfarm, in the most desolate part of the mountains where the snowcrust began. It was unthinkable to go on. Thank God, we found a cabin that was unlocked. There was a stove in one corner; we made a fire and stayed in the cabin overnight.

"The next day we continued. Good weather took us by surprise and melted the crust. I was wading through snow that reached up to my thigh, trudging forward a yard at a time. I was carrying a knapsack made of skins on my back, and with each step I sank in deep and struggled desperately to get back up. I struggled on like this for more than six miles. We got to Skjellavollen, where another small cabin saved us. Food was getting scarce and I was worried about how this trek over the mountains would end.

"I calculated that the third day would be the worst. I was right. It was approximately nineteen miles over treeless mountains to Smekkjolbua. There was not a single bush to be seen. We found our way by following the tops of some small stone markers which stuck up above the snow. I kept sinking down into the deep drifts, having to find enough strength each time to pull myself up. I was soaked with snow and sweat, my stockings were ripped and my courage was ebbing.

"We reached Smekkjolbua at dusk—there was a small cabin. The door had blown away, and a huge snowdrift had piled up on the floor. A few yards from the cabin, I just couldn't go on any longer. I was completely drained of strength; my mind went blank, overcome by a sense of utter hopelessness. I gave up, lay down in the mounded snow, and said to Big Karl: 'I can't take one more step.' He answered seriously: 'If I must sell my life, I shall sell it dearly....'

"Surprisingly, Big Karl's words cheered me up. I was not going to end *here*. I crawled through the snow masses, feeling as if my heart and every blood vessel were bursting, and got myself into the cabin. Big Karl made a fire. Lying on a pallet soaking wet, I felt warmth returning, and with it, the courage to live. We would make it. Undset in Ovre Rendal was only nine miles away and there we would be safe.

"On the fourth day, things started to improve. We were moving, heading downhill toward where people lived. Never in my life have I been happier to see a small bush growing. We had reached the tree line. When I saw the top of a pine above the snow, I knew that once again a Higher Power had been on my side.

"Just above the little hamlet called Undset, I

sat down in the snow, wringing out my stockings till the water streamed from them. I felt good, thinking about old Anne Kvernengen down in the village—I knew I could count on her help. She let me rest in bed for a whole day in her house. I was very cold, but still I felt as if I was melting after having been turned into a solid block of ice. Big Karl showed the effects of that trek over the mountains for a long time afterward. He didn't say much, was more serious than usual, and his face was deathly pale. For once, I think he was scared by something he had done."

On a clear fall day a couple of years later, Anna and Big Karl were trudging along the road in Ovre Rendal on one of their usual roving expeditions. Anna liked this area and felt like staying there awhile. Big Karl didn't care one way or the other. What was important to him was that Anna should earn enough so that he could get drunk and go off on his own now and then. As usual, Anna had to make the arrangements. She became a lumberjack in Saetanlia, bought an ax and a saw, and got her tools ready herself. There was an old camp up in the woods. She moved in there with Big Karl. Every day for weeks, she had to walk for an hour and a half through the forest to get to the logging area over roadless, difficult terrain.

"Around Christmas time, we had to move to

Sagkoia—a broken-down cabin with a bad stove. The nights were so cold that I looked forward to dawn and another trudge farther into the woods with my ax and saw. All day long I cut timber and stripped it of bark and twigs. The snow was deep, reaching up to my waist. At the end of the day, the only thing to do was to make a fire and sit in front of the stove. I had nothing to change into, so I'd sit in my working clothes, wet with snow and sweat, and let them dry. You were tired after a day like that, so it wasn't difficult to fall asleep, even though the pallet was hard and I had almost nothing to cover myself with.

"One day after the Christmas season when the weather was below zero, my feet got frostbitten while I was felling and stripping timber in the deep snow up in Saetanlia. I didn't realize what had happened until I was back in the cabin that evening. After I had started the fire in the stove, my left foot began to ache terribly. It was burning worst of all in the toes. The pain was unbearable but I knew the world was hard and pitiless, so I clamped my teeth together, saying to myself: 'You must get through this one, too, Anna.' I also thought: 'Nothing is ever so black that you can't find one small ray of light.' I remembered that a few days earlier there had been a timber-measuring and one of the men working the logs had complimented me on a job well done. That made me proud and made the work seem easier. It was a good thing to think about in the dark cabin with the winter night outside the window and the faint glow of red-hot embers shining through the stove door. I thought of something else too: If things had been the way they should have been between Big Karl and me, we could have talked about this. That would have helped. I kept everything to myself—we had nothing that we shared. He made demands and took from me, I gave without protest. I felt more and more like a tool in his hand, a kind of working machine; nothing human seemed to remain in the life I led.

"The next day I limped back into the woods. To stay in the cabin with Big Karl would have been the worst thing I could have done at that point. Everything would have hurt and my nerves wouldn't have been able to stand it. I couldn't wear shoes because my foot was so sore and swollen. Old Anne Kvernengen had given me a sock with soles made out of a felt hat—it came in handy now. I used that slipper in the timber forest for the rest of the winter.

"I got frost bumps on my foot that winter and my legs have never been quite right ever since. Every time the frost bumps hurt too much, I think about Anne Kvernengen—she was a kind and giving old woman. I think she froze more during her lifetime than I have. When she was still a child, her life was already cold and brutal. She sat in her tiny cottage and talked about herself often.

"One Christmas Eve when she was only a few years old, there was nothing at all to eat in her home. Her mother was in tears of desperation. She asked Anne and her sister to go down to the village in Rendalen, to beg Minister Bull, the father of Jacob Breda Bull, for a loan from God. Bull had understood that it was serious, his heart was in the right place, so Anne and her sister came home with food packages that dark Christmas Eve.

"I think Anne Kvernengen's childhood was worse than mine. She wasn't very old when she was sold at an auction in Rendalen—the lowest bidder got her. Those were the rules governing paupers at the time; whoever was willing to take over a child for the lowest amount of relief money from the public was sure to get one. It meant cheap labor for the bidder. A youngster sold at an auction had to be prepared for hard work and much humiliation. Anne Kvernengen found that out. That is why she started dreaming of having something of her own early in life. She wanted to be able to decide for herself what she would do with her day and with what was hers, little as that might be. She ended up living alone in the tiny cottage in Rendalen. That is where I met her; we became friends and she always helped me out when things were worst.

"Anne died as she had lived. It happened on a freezing cold winter's day. She was on her way to the cow shed to look after the animals. She was trudging along with a lantern in her hand. She was old by now and didn't always know what she was doing, so she went in the wrong direction. She somehow got onto a road used by lumberjacks and didn't know which way it led. She fell in the snow and lay there, stretched out in the cold night. A lumberjack found her; she was frozen stiff; there was almost no life left in her. She was taken to the old people's home in Rendalen. She died there soon after."

As soon as spring arrived, Big Karl refused to remain in Rendalen. He was tired of life in the lonely cabin and felt like taking to the highway again. He knew Anna had a little money and took it from her. The next few days, he was mainly out getting drunk. He and Anna walked with no particular goal in mind. By the end of April, they had gone all the way to the mountainous regions near Somadalen; Lake Ister lay to the east and the Femund mountains loomed on the horizon toward Sweden.

"Once again we were completely broke. Big Karl had spent our money on drink—we had nothing to eat and I had no new clothes. I looked awful and dreaded each day that lay ahead—the only bright thing was spring. It comes late in these parts. Still, when the sun was actually warm for a few short moments in the middle of the day, it was like a new gift of health.

"We knew of a miserable little fishing cabin near Fjerdingshaugen down by Lake Ister. It was situated four and a half miles to the north of Haugsetvolden—the lonely old mountain farm on the slope to the west of the lake. From Somadalen, there was no road down to the cabin. We trudged through the snow and were dead-tired when we reached the lakeside. The door was open, a rusty stove stood at an angle in one corner, and hard wooden pallets without mattresses or blankets were attached to the wall. The roof was neglected and ravaged by the wind—you could see daylight right through it. We crept inside to rest in these miserable surroundings.

"I would just as soon forget the days we spent in the fishing cabin near Fjerdingshaugen. I was so exhausted and hungry that I felt dizzy and couldn't think straight. There was no way we could get farther into the mountains. We were cut off, since there was no road. Things could not have been blacker—nothing seemed certain any more. Life didn't offer much, and there was no one to encourage me. We sat around silently hour after hour, without hope.

"After Big Karl and I had been in the fishing cabin for a few days, a couple of fellows drove up behind a horse and came to a halt. The men were old Jo Haugsetvolden and his son Johan, who had been gathering horse manure from the farms nearby. I could tell they were surprised to find people in the cabin. They also seemed to understand how bad things were. When Jo Haugsetvolden got up to go out to his horse, he suddenly stopped, looked at me for a long time with a fixed expression, and said: 'Tomorrow, you will come to my place. . . .'

"That turned out to be a decisive moment. I could hear his words over and over in my head and I knew that it was now or never.

"I went to Haugsetvolden the next day, April 30, 1928. It was four and a half miles over the frozen lake. I was in water and slush up to my knees and often went right through the ice. My ragged clothes got even more torn and I arrived at Haugsetvolden in a state of dazed exhaustion. No one could have felt poorer or more lost than I did the day I came up from the frozen lake to Haugsetvolden, with my hands still sore from cutting timber in Rendalen and swollen from struggling through the snow. It also pained me that I was not rid of Big Karl. He followed me to Haugsetvolden and settled there."

"The people who lived on Haugsetvolden at that time were Jo Haugsetvolden and his wife Tyri, their son Johan, and a half-brother of Jo's whom we called

ANNA

Old-Johan—he lived alone in a fishing cabin at the edge of the lake. The first few days, I often sat in the old-fashioned main room at Haugsetvolden, watching the people who lived there: Jo was a big strong man, he looked like someone who made demands on himself and on others—he had clearly become hardened by the rugged life he had led. Tyri was old and small and worn by her rough life on the land. When she walked, she bent over so much that her head almost touched her knees. She was dressed in sackcloth and, whenever she looked up, her head was cocked to one side. She did not look kind, I was half scared of her; she threw the food at me as if I were a dog. It was her way of doing things and the food didn't taste good that way. I felt as if I hadn't done what was expected of me, even though I did the hardest work on Haugsetvolden from the very first day. I dreaded each bite of food that was going to be thrown.

"I didn't feel particularly at home. Everything was so different from what I was used to. I was in no way spoiled, but I had searched for security ever since childhood and didn't think I would settle down in this place. It felt cold in every way. There were two rooms for four people—they were messy, dirty, and had the smell of poverty about them. Even so, I hoped I could remain at Haugsetvolden. I had decided that I was finished with the wandering life. I didn't want to take to the road ever again and this couldn't be worse than that had been.

"It didn't look at all as if Big Karl intended to leave Haugsetvolden. Now that I knew what I wanted, I was determined to do it, no matter what. Big Karl understood that I was serious when I said to him: 'I am not coming with you anymore. I suffered enough because of you; I don't want to see you ever again. I am staying at Haugsetvolden.'

"Right after that, Jo Haugsetvolden asked Big Karl to disappear. I was listening from a distance. Even though I was prepared for almost anything from Big Karl, the last hours I spent with him were the hardest and most painful of all. I had never dreamt that a human being could be exploited up to the very last minute, the way it happened to me. I stood there and heard how Big Karl sold me to Haugsetvolden. He argued with Jo about the price and I watched Jo pay three hundred kroner for me. Big Karl had always taken from me whatever I owned and in return he sold me like a slave.

"Big Karl left Haugsetvolden early the next morning. The lake had risen during the night and Johan rowed him over to Fjerdingshaugen.

"I watched from the window at Haugsetvolden as he moved out of sight on the north side of the lake. The story of my life with him ended then and there. He went east, over the border to Sweden. I heard later that he died in a hospital in Mora."

3

"In the early days of my stay at Haugsetvolden, I almost gave up. It became clear that I was expected to be a combination of horse, man, and woman—more was asked of me than I could handle. Also I couldn't stand Tyri throwing the food at me; I simply couldn't swallow it while she was in the same room.

"One day, when I was really depressed, I lay down on the ground next to the old storeroom, desperate and hungry. I had no more strength left and could see nothing worth living for. I dug my fingers into the earth and hid my face in the grass. That day, I believe the earth answered.

"I suddenly folded my hands together and prayed. I turned on my back, looking right up at the sky, and asked out loud: 'What am I to do, where am I to go?' It was a prayer and a challenge. Then it was as if I heard a voice saying to me: 'You must stay *here* on Haugsetvolden. The people here need you. The people at Haugsetvolden cannot live in these mountains without your help. Anna, your duty lies here.' The words I heard most clearly of all were: 'Go thou forth and perform the deeds that are written in God's law. . . .'

"From that moment on, I was no longer in doubt. Hereafter, I would live my life on Haugsetvolden, in the wilderness. The road ahead was clear."

At Haugsetvolden, Anna had to participate in all kinds of work. Her sex was never taken into account; she was never asked how much she could handle. People who were familiar with the situation at Haugsetvolden at that time used to say: "Jo takes better care of his horse than of Anna—Anna does the work that the horse is spared."

Anna never thought of going easy on herself. She was certain that her help was essential for the survival of the family. She kept reminding herself that the person to be pitied was the one who had no opportunity to help his fellow man. Poverty almost broke her in the logging cabin in Rendalen and in the fishing cabin in Fjerdingshaugen, but that was only a bad memory now. She felt that helping others gave meaning to her life. When everything seemed at its worst, she thought of Martinus Somaen —the old mailman who came to Haugsetvolden once a week. In the summer he first traveled six miles down to Lake Ister, then rowed ten miles to Glotberget. Covered with ice and snow, in the winter he walked through the mountains, carrying his mailbag and often some birds he'd just caught as well. Martinus laughed at anything that appeared hard or wrong. Nothing bothered him; he was inured to life in the wilderness.

"I also remembered things I had heard about my own mother. She wasn't strong enough to breast-feed me when I was born, so she rubbed soot on her nipples to make me stop sucking. When I remembered that, it wasn't difficult for me to keep quiet.

"Toward the end of June we moved to the *seter* up the mountain, seven miles from Haugsetvolden. I stayed with the animals in the woods and the mountains all day long. I carried a bag full of rags on my back—every hour had to be used to the full. While I walked, I kept the knitting needles going; I knitted socks, mittens, shirts, and scarves for Jo and Johan. When I was sitting down, I mended their ragged old clothes. Tyri sent some food along with me, but it was far from adequate and when I returned to the *seter* in the evening I was always starving. However, before any food appeared on the table, I had to milk the cows and do the evening chores.

"I got a special pleasure from minding the goats, even though the work was often lonely. Sometimes the loneliness was a great fear that filled me completely. I was surrounded by nature and everything seemed overwhelming, impossible to grasp. I had only the animals to turn to. Several times I experienced an inexplicably close contact with them. I often lay close to a cow, with my head against its neck, and felt warm and safe, as though we'd always be together.

"There were many fine days with sunshine on the moors and occasional gentle breezes. At such times, I'd find myself humming a catchy, old-fashioned dance tune. The strange thing was that this always happened when I was on my way home through Svalskaret. This spot was more protected than the rest of the mountain—and the fragrances of heather, birch, and juniper were stronger here than anywhere else. The animals and I enjoyed the area, and the flock followed me in perfect formation. We shared the same rhythm and moved in unison toward home.

"One summer there was a vicious bull on

Haugsetvolden. I was scared to death of the bull and went around with a big, heavy stick. Near Svalbua I thought my last hour had come. I had no warning that anything was about to happen, when the bull suddenly knocked me down. The stick fell out of my hand and I was left defenseless. I remained face down on the ground, not making a move, as if I were dead. The bull prodded with his horns again and again and trampled me underfoot until my clothes were ripped to shreds. His horns felt like awls in my back but I clenched my fists and didn't make a sound. He breathed hard and scraped the ground, making earth and bits of moss fly about. But then he calmed down and ambled away. That evening I came home exhausted and upset. I was sore and black and blue for a long time afterward. The vicious bull had to pay with his life for that nonsense near Svalbua.

"During the day, while I minded the goats, Jo and Johan cut hay near the cottage. It was my job to drag the hay over to the drying frames. This I did in the evening after I was through with the chores in the cow shed. I worked late many a summer night."

Although the work was hard, Anna didn't mind. She had a feel for the summer nights and enjoyed being alone in the mountains. She felt that there was something special about such a time—it smelled nice, there were sounds that aroused her curiosity and a swarming life all around that made the hours interesting. The birds that flew around her seemed as busy as she was.

"I would smile at the sight of little birds working hard to take care of themselves and their families. You are a kind of bird too, Anna, I thought—you too have a family to take care of.

"Best of all, I liked comparing myself to a woodpecker. Sometimes I sat on a mound near the *seter* with the rake in my lap, vividly recalling a story my mother had told me when I was a little girl: While Jesus was still wandering among us here on earth, one day when he was hungry he came to a woman baking bread. The woman's name was Gjertrud and she wore a red kerchief on her head. Jesus asked for a piece of bread. The woman took a small piece and it turned into a large loaf. She took smaller and smaller pieces, and the loaves got bigger and bigger, but she gave none at all to Jesus. So Jesus said: 'Because you would not give me even one piece of bread, you will turn into a bird that must find its bread between the bark and the wood. You will only have water when it rains.' Instantly, a bird flew out of the chimney, a bird with a red top—the woodpecker, or gjertrudsbird as we call it. I didn't understand the story very well when my mother told it to me, but now I do: Share the good things you have with others. The only good things I owned were my hands. I wanted to use them to help the people at Haugsetvolden."

Anna's hands were certainly needed. She worked on, year after year, summer and winter, often doing the heaviest chores at Haugsetvolden. When the hay had been stored inside the *seter,* she had to strike farther into the mountains to gather more fodder for the animals. She cut it with her scythe miles away from home, in the open meadows, around small lakes, and alongside little brooks. She also found grass to cut in the big, wet moors and deep swamps. She stacked all her cuttings on frames, layer upon layer. On top she put the "water roof"; she used the tallest grass for that and it took a lot of effort to build. As soon as it got cold, when snow began to fall and the ice was strong enough, what had been cut had to be brought home. It was nearly ten miles from Haugsetvolden to Setertjonna, in the mountains, where most of the marshy grass was cut. To bring it down required Jo and Johan as well as Anna. They drove down to Isterendholmen with horse and sleigh over ice that was often dangerous. They continued westward on land, through treacherous fields where it was easy to get stuck.

"Many times it was so bad that I thought we would all have to give up. There was nothing to do but take a chance—if you didn't, you soon lost. We'd either make it or we wouldn't—and most of the time we made it. It semed like a miracle each time we found a way out when the situation looked utterly hopeless. Ever since I was a child, I have believed that everything would collapse if I lost my conviction that what I was doing would work."

Fall and winter were the most difficult seasons for everyone on Haugsetvolden, especially for Anna. She had to help old Tyri in the house, mornings and evenings. Her days were spent doing a man's work alongside Jo and Johan. Starting late in October and during most of November, Anna was up in the mountains, in Svalasen and Svalskaret, gathering moss. It had to be loaded up into huge piles weighing about 650 pounds each. It was common to put up eight to ten loads a day.

"To gather the moss, I used a common pitchfork. Then I carried the moss on my back in a basket to where we had made a solid base for a load. All winter I went along when the loads were being driven home from the mountain. To prepare for these trips, I'd ski into the woods with my snowshoes thrown over my shoulders, a few days ahead of time. I went alone to make the trail on the marshland. I left tracks until water showed above the snow and on my shoes. Sometimes I fainted, but I knew I *had* to do this—it meant safeguarding the lives of the people and the animals on Haugsetvolden. When it got cold, the tracks I had made on the marshes became roads we could drive on. That's when I'd feel a pang of something joyful within me.

"The toughest days in the mountains began with the snows. They could be so deep that we could see nothing but the horse's back. I often had to walk in front with my ax to cut down stumps that were in the way. Several times the horse would get stuck in snowdrifts, exhausted and completely soaked in snow and sweat. I'd take the spade and dig around the horse's feet to free them, so he could take the next step. A little farther, it would be just as bad again—the horse stuck once more along with the heavy load of moss. At other times, the horse simply collapsed and I had to dig the snow out from under him, so he could stand up again. I always felt that the horse was worse off than I was. That helped me to carry on. People who love animals and have worked with a horse are wonderfully strong and enduring when it is a matter of life and death. I wouldn't have worked harder for my own child than I did for the horse. We were both in distress, in danger. I must admit that when things appeared most threatening, I was reminded of what happened to Hallstein Nyvoll of Narbuvoll. One winter he was alone in these mountains and a load of moss collapsed on him. When he was found, he was dead and his horse was standing nearby, pining and frozen in the deep snow.

ANNA

"I often drove to the mountains alone with horse and sleigh. At the end of October it was I who drove the moss home because Johan was fishing the bottom of Lake Ister. The horse Blakken and I had to manage alone. I raked the moss right onto the sleigh, stamping it down as much as I could, so as to get as much as possible home at one time. It wasn't any good to come back from the mountain with just a little moss. Tyri would take it out on both Blakken and me. The horse seemed to understand me; each time I got up on the load to stamp on it, he tossed his head gaily. He seemed to be encouraging me, seemed to say: 'Stamp on it again, Anna, we can manage a few more shovels full!'

"No matter how well I knew the mountains, I wasn't always sure where I was. Sudden snowfalls changed the landscape. Storms set in while Blakken and I were out fetching the moss. I never even considered turning back; it would have been regarded as a disgrace on Haugsetvolden. The ax came in handy on days like that. I cut nicks in the trees on the way out, to make sure I could find my way home again. Many times I was so grateful for those white marks on the tree trunks; they made me feel secure when Blakken and I drove home to Haugsetvolden in near darkness.

"I felt like a wet, bedraggled crow when I returned from the moss mountain and put Blakken in the stable. As soon as I left the horse, I felt alone. He seemed to be the only one I could rely on. But I also felt that I was *receiving* something at times like that, that someone was trying to make me happy.

"Every piece of moss I distributed to the animals gave me real satisfaction. It was a kind of blessing to have gathered and brought home the moss that meant so unbelievably much to the poor animals, chained in the stalls of the cow shed.

"And another thing: the warmth from the cows was the best. It cut right through the heavy, wet rags I had on and got to the body underneath. When I finished my chores in the cow shed in the evening and closed the door, I always felt that a good, meaningful day had ended."

When March and April appeared on the calendar at Haugsetvolden, Anna got ready to cut wood. Usually, she went over the ice on Lake Ister to Digerneset, where there was excellent timber. As soon as she was finished with her chores on Haugsetvolden, she put the saw and the ax on a sled and was on her way. If there was too little snow on Lake Ister, she went on foot. The rest of the time, she put on her skis and went east. When the weather was good, she stopped on the ice; she was happy to feel the sun growing warmer with each passing day. The Femund mountains took on a bluish cast and she knew the reindeer were about somewhere over on Bjonnberget. She liked thinking of them; it added some life to the monotonous snowy landscape. The empty spaces around Haugsetvolden became more exciting and lively. She never permitted herself to stop for more than a few minutes to take a breather or just to daydream; her daily work required all her time.

"There was a lot of fine dry pine on Digerneset. We call it dry 'gadd,' and it was excellent for the stove at Haugsetvolden. I put the wood I had cut on the sled and pulled it through the snow down to the lake's edge. Later I went and got it with Blakken. I often tasted blood as I strained to pull the big logs to the lake. It was hard on my back too, so it was no wonder that it hurt when I went to bed at night. I had to think of something that would take my mind off how I felt. It always helped to think of the old cottage women in Hedmark. As a very young girl, I went along to tie bundles at the large farms at harvest time. The old cottage women never enjoyed doing this kind of work—I could understand why. But I always wondered why they didn't try to be more lighthearted and good-humored about it. I often saw that they would rather cry, and that made me *laugh*. They misunderstood that. I was given a hard time about laughing, but there was something inside me that hated tears at harvest time. We were

Every day Anna stands by the window
at Haugsetvolden, looking down over the lake
and mountains to the east.

———————————————

Anna stands on the spot where a widow and her children built the first house on the hill one hundred and forty years before.

There is a special feeling to the farm's dark, leaning wooden buildings.

From the courtyard at Haugsetvolden the land slopes away to the lake and the wilderness beyond.

Anna handles an ax as well as any man,
having had to chop wood and cut timber for the
family on Haugsetvolden since her youth.

Anna has had to learn self-sufficiency.
If anything needs sharpening, she must turn
the heavy whetting stone herself.

Sunday on Haugsetvolden. This horse has been
her faithful companion through the years;
together they have had to make
countless journeys through the wilderness.

Ola Sorhus

handling our daily bread and I could never bring myself to complain about that.

"I went to cut wood all around Haugsetvolden. We used up a lot of it. The buildings were old and cold and no one can imagine how much raw birchwood I have chopped and brought home. I often used the log saw. When I did, Johan came with me and we attacked the really big ones. The log saw meant hard work, but Johan was understanding. He had suffered a lot himself and he knew all about it. He'd 'take five' as a matter of course without wanting me to know he did it for my sake. In general we said very little. We understood each other very well and that sufficed.

"I made many trips with the horse during the winter to get birch twigs for the cattle. I chopped the twigs into little pieces and gave them to the cows. It was meager fodder, but the animals liked it. None of the cows on Haugsetvolden got an infected udder or milking fever, thanks to the birch twigs. They help prevent illness.

"Blakken and I left in the morning and went in a westerly direction toward the hilly region around Lake Ormuttu to find the birch twigs. It could happen that we didn't return until the middle of the night. I chopped the twigs by moonlight and was in a world of my own, in a way, far from any road and with only Blakken for company. There weren't many surprises, so I thought it was fun and a great adventure if a fox appeared in front of us while we drove along Lake Ormuttu by the light of the moon.

"The people on Haugsetvolden didn't like my staying out late at night when I was fetching birch twigs from the mountains. Old Tyri crouched on the edge of her bed with the light filtering through the cracks of the stove door. She was unpleasant and worried, but she never asked how *I* was—she wondered if such long trips were not too much for Blakken.

"We had our worst springtime pinch at Haugsetvolden during the war. We were well prepared; I had chopped lots of twigs because we knew the procurement officers might come any day and take our hay. And that's exactly what happened. In the spring three men came and went straight to the barn. They started weighing the hay and making up a load. The load got bigger and bigger and the hay bin shrank and we got scared. I didn't think much about the work I had done getting the hay from the moors in the mountains—I was too afraid for the animals. Things looked really bad. If we couldn't save the animals, we didn't have much of a chance. I couldn't restrain myself, I went right up to the men and told them straight to their faces: 'You are taking our hay.

All we have left on Haugsetvolden are birch twigs. You can come and stand on twigs and see how it tastes.'

"I felt better having said that. When the men swayed out of the barn, across the grounds and through the gate with the load of hay, I had already made up my mind that not even that would finish us. The birch twigs were all we could count on; they had saved us on Haugsetvolden before, when everything looked bad. We'd find a way out this time, too. In my mind, the war and birch twigs have gone together ever since. I can thank the birch twigs for a great deal."

4

The people on Haugsetvolden did their big trading twice a year. They drove all the way to Roros, sixty-two miles from Lake Ister. Anna often took part in these difficult journeys in winter. Each trip took a week and Blakken had to pull heavy loads both coming and going. When Anna and Johan left Haugsetvolden, the load consisted of grouse, big birds, pink trout, and furs. It was mainly a matter of bartering. These goods were exchanged for several sacks of flour, one whole case of refined sugar plus bags of regular sugar, salt, cereal, dried peas, and coffee. Anna had been there when the grouse and the trout were caught that were part of the load she was taking to Roros. There were more than 100 grouse and 150 pounds of frozen trout.

"There is one trip to Roros I will never forget. Johan and I were on our way home with a heavy load, as usual. We stayed overnight in Hadalen. We got up early—we knew what we were getting into because the Korsode mountain was covered with deep snow. It was even worse than we had anticipated. Blakken kept sinking into the snow until only his back was visible. Johan and I had to keep digging; we freed the horse several times. Moving in spurts, we managed to get across the mountain. Whenever Blakken couldn't make it any longer, we shoveled the snow out of the way so that he could tread on solid ground. We also had to roll some 220-pound sacks off the load occasionally, to give him a chance to pull forward a few more feet. Johan and I followed behind with the sacks, bent double, stumbling and falling. We strained every muscle and, God knows how, managed to lift the sacks back onto the load. Blakken took a few more steps and we slid forward again.

"We reached Holda in the evening and stayed overnight. The next day we went through Tufsingdalen to Femund. The lake had begun to thaw and we got stuck. We were facing Buvika when it happened. The horse understood the seriousness of the situation and became very restless. He was terribly scared and kept digging in with his feet. He yanked and jerked so much that finally the shafts broke off.

"There we were. All we could do was try and get to Buvika. We unharnessed the horse and started out on the frozen lake. We left behind the load of food, which all of us on Haugsetvolden were meant to live on for the next few months. It looked as if a huge animal had collapsed on the ice. It was getting dark and we still had miles to go before we'd reach Buvika and people. When we got there, they were very helpful. They let us stay overnight, and the next day they lent us shafts for the horse.

"That day was one of hard work and great difficulties. We were on the stretch to Jota in Somadalen. It had snowed a lot the night before and we couldn't see the road. We struggled on, shoveling snow until we couldn't see straight. We were just about worn out. But I knew from past experience that when something *has* to be done, when something really serious is at stake, there's always a way out. We did last through it, Blakken, Johan, and I. When we got home, Tyri for once seemed more kind and gentle than I had ever noticed before."

"The last shopping expedition Johan and I made to Roros took place in April 1936. The route over Femund was impassable. People had warned us against taking it, so we took the mountain road to Oversjodalen. A few days later, we were on our way home from Roros with an especially big, heavy load. A terrible storm hit us as we were climbing the Oversjodal mountains, which are steep and ugly. The sky was the color of lead and it was snowing as if the heavens had opened. We still had twelve miles to go. Snow whipped in our faces, it *stung* so much that we couldn't keep our eyes open. It was so thick that you couldn't see your hand in front of your face anyhow.

"Johan and I stumbled along behind the load. We saw the horse only faintly—he looked like a dark gray ghost. This was a notoriously dangerous road. Horses had been known to fall over the cliff, and we started to worry. We agreed that we had to keep our spirits up. Giving up meant death, not only for Johan, Blakken, and me, but also for the people on Haugsetvolden who were helpless and depended on us in every way. That night, we had to pit our strength against all the forces of nature in the Oversjodal mountains. Every inch gained in the snow was a victory.

"Around midnight, we made out a few houses through the blizzard. We had arrived at Svarthaugen, a lonely farm in the mountains. They knew us from previous trips, but they were sure to be scared at having unexpected arrivals in the middle of this stormy night. It was a matter of life and death for man and horse, so I gave a loud knock on the door.

"At first, the people at Svarthaugen didn't recognize us, we looked so exhausted and wretched. They thought a band of Gypsies had lost their way. Mountain people have always been ready to help, and we had ample proof of it that awful night in the Oversjodals.

"I guess I was spared that night because there still remained too much on Haugsetvolden for me to do."

5

Every winter during the war, Anna drove horse-drawn loads between Somadalen and Femundsenden. It was a distance of nineteen miles and she did it all by herself. Many times the work was beyond human endurance. People who saw her and the horse bring the loads through snowstorms and freezing weather over the frozen lake or on narrow trails in the woods thought she was mad. Anna never thought so. The important thing for her was to keep everyone alive on Haugsetvolden. She knew all about this country, in all seasons of the year. She knew what to do and had been tested so often by now that she was no longer afraid of the storms and the freezing cold. She had to bring coffee, sugar, flour, and all the other staples that could be had to her people in the mountains. She was prepared to do her share—she considered it her duty to see to it that the goods reached their destination.

Early in the morning, she hitched Blakken to the front of the sleigh; she drove along Lake Ister and on to Femundsenden. There she lifted a load weighing hundreds of pounds onto the sleigh and, in the evening, drove back to Haugsetvolden. The next day, she drove to the store in Somadalen, unloaded, and returned home the same evening. The old people and the animals were waiting for her there—they needed her care.

"One winter's day, such a big storm started blowing while I was building a big load in Femundsenden that I decided to stay overnight. It would have been senseless to take horse and load onto Lake Ister and travel north in the direction of Haugsetvolden. Thank God, I had brought some hay along for the horse; during the war it wasn't easy to find such things on short notice. The next morning, when I was going to feed him and get ready to drive on, I discovered the Germans or somebody had taken the hay. There was absolutely none left. I didn't know what to do, but I was determined to do something. I picked some composition boards off the floor of the cow shed where the horse was standing. The boards were wet and full of manure. I had a few pieces of fish that had gone sour in my provision bag. I cooked them, put them on the boards, and tempted the horse with this. Blakken decided that enough was enough, he absolutely refused to touch what I had to offer him. He looked at me, puzzled and reproachful, but there was nothing else I could do.

"He hadn't eaten a thing when I put the shafts on him, gave him a pat to tell him to go, and said: 'We'll have a try at it, Blakken. You might be a little pleased to know that I left one 220-pound bag behind for the next time.'

"When we got to Haugsetvolden with the load, I don't know which of us was more worn out. That was one day that made me especially glad I had brought the grass from the marshland down the mountain. Blakken didn't exactly get any war rations in his stall after the trip."

"Another time during the war years, just before Christmas, some people from another area had come to Elvalsvollen, the old fishing station east of Lake Ister, three miles from Northern Somaen. I had been to Somadalen with a load; night had overtaken me because of the snow and bad sleighing conditions. I was asked to drive some provisions from Somadalen down to Northern Somaen, where these people would come and get them.

"This trip in the dead of night could easily have meant serious trouble for Blakken and me. I didn't want to refuse to drive for the people in Elvalsvollen; in a few days it would be Christmas and this was what they were going to subsist on. There was no decent road, just a small trail, so it was hard going, and slow. When we got down to Somaa, something happened that I have never understood since. Blakken suddenly wouldn't go any farther; he stood stock still and refused to budge an inch. A moment later, he suddenly swung round and galloped wildly up the hill, scared out of his wits and completely out of control. I didn't let go of the reins, so I was knocked down and pulled along behind the sleigh through the deep snow like a bundle of rags. We crashed through the woods and I was unable to stop him until we were back on the road a few hundred yards from Somaa. He was foaming at the mouth and shaking all over. I did my best to calm him down, patted him, talked to him and, as soon as I dared, ordered him forward. The horse obeyed, but he was still excited and uneasy.

"Not far from where this happened, there was a lonely farm in the woods called Ronningen. I drove there and knocked on the door. Karl Larsson understood the situation at once; he was used to horses and was able, more or less, to calm Blakken down. I left the goods for Elvalsvollen behind at Ronningen—it made no sense for me to make another attempt to go there. The people in Ronningen didn't want to send us on our way that awful night. But I knew what they would think at Haugsetvolden if I didn't show up, so we started toward home, hoping that the fates were on our side.

"Blakken was in good shape again now, he knew the road and understood that the next stop was his stable. I wrapped the few clothes I had on more tightly around me and tried to find consolation in the beauty of the winter's night in the forest. It was not the right time for that. I got no pleasure out of the clearings, the large rocks I knew by name, or the huts we drove past. They were just there; they proved that we were on the right road.

"It was the next morning by the time Blakken and I reached Haugsetvolden. It was dark and the crooked old houses ahead of us looked like the home of some kind of trolls. It felt good and safe to see them. I put Blakken in the stable and just managed to have a catnap before the next day's work began. I had to get up early, the cattle were waiting for my morning rounds."

ANNA

One freezing day in winter, around noon, Anna was washing the dishes at Haugsetvolden. It was so cold that the logs were cracking, and each time Tyri or Jo came in through the door, gusts of cold and steam poured into the room. Johan had taken the horse to Lake Ormuttu for wood. Anna felt sorry for both of them when they left; the sleigh runners creaked on the snow and you could see the horse's breath steaming out of his mouth as they drove through the gateway and disappeared to the west.

"Suddenly all hell broke loose. Johan ran loudly through the hallway, yanked open the door and collapsed on the floor, terrified and covered with frost. 'I've driven the horse into the lake. Now we're done for here on Haugsetvolden,' he said.

"I knew what I had to do. I grabbed a hatchet and ran as fast as I could to the lake, more than a mile away. I had been there for quite a while before Johan arrived, scared and breathless. He had struggled back alone as best he could. Blakken had gone through the ice far from the shore and now he was in so deep that only his back showed above the surface. I tried to get his front feet up on the ice, but he kept pulling them back down as soon as I had them up there. I grabbed his collar and yanked as hard as I could. Nothing worked. Johan and I were frantic, and the horse stood strangely still in the icy water of the lake.

" 'I'm going to dash to Somadalen for help,' I said. 'You'll have to manage as best you can, Johan.'

"I was light on my feet as I ran the miles to get help. The crew didn't get Blakken out of the lake until eleven o'clock at night. They got him up on one side and Johan and I and everybody else sighed with relief.

"Then we suddenly were seized with fear all over again. The horse lay on the ice completely motionless, there was no sign of life. Everything had been in vain, and Haugsetvolden was a great deal poorer than before. But Martin Langsjoen from Somadalen refused to give up. We were not to let the horse get all stiff, he needed massage and warmth. When things looked their worst, Blakken surprised us all—he got up on his legs and swayed forward on the ice toward land.

"Johan and I were worn out for a long time afterward. We had huge blisters on our hands from having dug around in the water of the lake for hours. We both got frostbite and the mittens we wore were as stiff as bark. Johan's hands never recovered completely. I was wearing rubber boots which were full of water and I had no feeling in my feet for a long time afterward.

"We never mentioned this at Haugsetvolden when anybody talked about what had happened that day. I handled it my way and said I had carried home a lot of ice from Lake Ormuttu the night Blakken was saved. I always added that my skirt stood on the floor on the main room by itself, like a barrel."

Until a few years ago, the skull of a bear hung on the wall of the pantry at Haugsetvolden. The bear was shot to the west on the mountain a hundred years ago, and Anna more than once heard Jo Haugsetvolden tell the story of how the bear was killed.

"It happened around midsummer. Per Bolstad, a young boy from Rendalen, was on his way over the mountain to Haugsetvolden. He had a permit for Lake Ister and he was going fishing. The young lad was alone and carried a shotgun, which was normal for people moving about in the mountains. Per Bolstad didn't have his mind on hunting, he was looking forward to the big fish in Lake Ister. He was the kind of fellow who liked walking in the mountains, preferably alone, as often as he could. Evenings in a fishing cabin and freshly caught salmon trout for breakfast were a special treat for him in the wilderness.

"Two miles west of Haugsetvolden, by Pulltjonna, he came upon a mother bear with her two cubs in the middle of the road. Per Bolstad moved fast. He knew that every second counted. He had always heard old people say that a mother bear with cubs was extremely dangerous. He didn't hesitate. He took aim, fired, and immediately started to run. He didn't dare look to see if he had hit anything. He was afraid the mother bear might only be wounded, in which case he could expect her claws in his back at any moment.

"The young boy ran for his life down to Haugsetvolden, where he met Jo and asked for a rifle. Jo Haugsetvolden didn't have any rifle at the time, so the two of them took the boat and rowed across Lake Ister to Saeterasen, about seven miles away, and borrowed a rifle from Anders Haugen.

"Two very excited fellows went west over the mountain to Pulltjonna with that rifle. They soon found out what had happened. The mother bear had died on the spot where Per Bolstad had hit her with his shotgun. She hadn't died right away; she had had time to prepare her deathbed from moss and heather. She was lying on it when the two of them got there. When Jo Haugsetvolden told the bear story, he always added that just before they arrived the cubs had been with the mother bear and emptied her of milk.

"Jo and the young boy from the west side of the mountain skinned the bear near Pulltjonna and carried the meat down to Haugsetvolden. Jo put the bear skull up on the pantry wall and it hung there for almost a hundred years. Then the Norwegian Museum of Forestry got the skull. It is kept there in memory of the times when there were still bears on Haugsetvolden."

Anna went along to hunt and to fish as a matter of course. Most of the time she went to the mountain or the lake with Johan, but in the winter she often went alone to catch grouse with snares.

Spring was a great time for Anna. Flocks of black grouse played on the frozen lake and fought until the feathers flew. Johan and Anna got up early when the spring gathering was in progress. They sneaked along the edge of the lake, crawling as close to the meeting ground as they could, clever as cats. At times like these they felt that life on Haugsetvolden was full of wonder.

"I looked forward to those spring mornings all year long. The flocking of the grouse was like a fairytale come true. Another great adventure for Johan and me was our yearly trip to Glofoken. We skied on crusty snow to where the wood grouse were certain to be. I made sure never to miss it. Johan and I made the trip for the experience and just to watch. We never thought of bringing a rifle along. The best time was at sunrise. The fierce, wild antics were in full swing and the light from the morning sun made the Rendal mountains shine. *That's* when I thought life and the meet were the way things ought to be.

"I enjoyed hunting grouse in the winter too. I did that by myself. I laid out snares in about twenty places and every other day I made a trip to see what I had caught. On these trips I went deep in the mountains and I usually brought home five or ten grouse. Even though we lived right in the middle of grouse country, we never ate any on Haugsetvolden. They were too good for us. Grouse were excellent to barter with; they belonged in the load when Johan and I were ready for the trip to Roros. We did eat the duck eggs I gathered at the end of May. I made nesting houses out of old hollowed-out fir tree stumps, hung them up in the trees, and, after a couple of days, I climbed up to see if there was anything to collect. I might collect as many as eighty-four duck eggs from the houses in a few days. Johan set a lot of steel traps and we caught hawks, falcons, great horned owls, and ordinary owls that way."

By the standards of Haugsetvolden, fishing brought in a good income. Anna was a natural at that too. The most tiring fishing was done in the fall, from October 25 until Christmas time. Anna and Johan often went fishing for fourteen days at a time. They started in the part of the lake nearest Haugsetvolden and moved on to the northern end, close to Elvalsvollen. That's when the work became most exhausting for Anna. She was not only looking for whitefish up north, she also had to care for the animals and the old people on Haugsetvolden. She skied back and forth from the farm to the old fishing station every morning and every evening.

"We left by the grayish light of dawn. I rowed the boat out and set out the nets. That late in the fall the weather is awful and it can change abruptly. Many times the waves broke over us, the boat heaved up and down and danced on the lake like a cork. When there were whitecaps, the rowing was hard work, but it was also the only way to keep warm.

"On landing in Elvalsvollen, I was soaked to the skin but I didn't have time to dry off in the cabin. First I had to clean the fish. It was common to catch eighty or ninety whitefish a day. As soon as I was finished cleaning the fish, I threw a large string of them over my shoulder and started back home to Haugsetvolden. I had to think of something while I walked, preferably something pleasant. Nothing was more pleasing than the thought of the animals waiting for me. I had come to depend on them, in a way. I looked forward to opening the door of the cow shed and being met with the lowing from the stalls. It gave me a sense of warmth, peace, and an indescribable security."

"Knowing how to handle a boat came in handy for more than fishing. In the early spring, as soon as it was possible to row across Lake Ister to Digerneset on the other side, I transported manure from Haugsetvolden. We couldn't grow potatoes on Haugsetvolden because the ground was frozen too much of the time, so we planted our potatoes on the east side of the lake. Mikkel Nilsen Somaaen plowed the first field in Digerneset as early as 1875. The people from Haugsetvolden plowed three. I did my share of that work too.

"I shoveled dung into sacks and carried them to the boat on the lake. A load usually consisted of ten sacks and it took me half an hour to row across the lake. When I got to Digerneset, I dumped the sacks ashore and carried them on my back to the furrows. I brought the seed potatoes in boxes, planted them in the barren soil, scattered the manure over them, and dug up more soil to pack around them. I had done my part and relied on the good Lord for the rest.

"Then came fall. The days I spent in Digerneset harvesting potatoes were different from other days. I could see results, and it made working easier than usual. Something useful had been accomplished.

"When I rowed home to Haugsetvolden in the evening, with the new potatoes in their boxes piled up high in the boat, I felt like rowing all around Lake Ister to show off my pride and joy. Everything I did seemed easy. I felt as if the world around me and the sky had to take notice of my treasure. I was richly rewarded for rowing dung and seed potatoes in the spring. I felt happy and grateful."

6

Old-Johan of Haugsetvolden was Jo's half-brother. Everybody always called him Old-Johan, and he was considered to be the most eccentric fellow in the Osterdal mountains. In a way, he didn't really belong with the people of Haugsetvolden. He had bought his own fishing license to the lake in 1902 and had built himself a small cabin at the lakeside. He lived there alone all his life, in one indescribably dirty little room. The furnishings consisted mainly of a bed, a stove, a small table, and a cupboard. The coffee pot was always on the stove; a spoon and a knife were stuck in a couple of cracks in the cabin wall. Heavy fishing nets hung on rough wooden plugs; a rusty sewing machine sat in a corner. The windows were small and dirty, with piles of dead flies on the windowsills. The light filtering into the fishing cabin was always grayish. Old-Johan was a self-sufficient type. He was never helpless. He knew how to deal with life in the wilderness around Haugsetvolden and Lake Ister.

It wasn't easy to get close to Old-Johan. He was suspicious of strangers, he had his own ways and wanted to be left alone. He didn't want anybody watching when he pushed his boat into the water and set out his nets. Old-Johan and the wilderness were as one, and would have no truck with disturbances. He had found his way of life and wanted no foreign tracks within his territory.

But Anna won Old-Johan's confidence. He permitted her to come inside his cabin. She always tried to be of help, although she knew beforehand that he would refuse to let her.

"Old-Johan's life in the cabin on Lake Ister was something completely out of the ordinary. I am thinking not only of his stark life-style, but of his capacity to take care of himself. He was a master at mending nets. While he was doing it, he had a small blade attached to his right index finger to cut off superfluous bits of thread without a pause. As he worked, he often sang a tune; he had a fine high voice and preferred the songs of Gjest Bardsen.

"Old-Johan with his unruly, messed-up head of hair and long, bristly beard was also his own tailor. Most of the time he wore clothes made of heavy lodencloth with a huge cape he had sewn from flour sacks he had dyed. The cape hung down almost to his ankles and was an uneven purplish blue. His legs were wrapped in strips he had cut from more sackcloth. He always wore these strips around his neck as well. He made himself a hat by getting hold of an old piece of worn-out cloth. He sewed it into a kind of bag for his head and took pieces of very wooly sheepskin, which he stitched on for the ears. He attached ribbons to the pieces of sheepskin, and when he went outside on a cold day in winter or went fishing on Lake Ister on a stormy fall day he tied these ribbons together in tight knots under his beard. At times like this he was stern and unapproachable.

"Old-Johan never bought clothes or shoes. On his shopping trips to Roros, he exchanged his fish for fur and leather. He made his own shoes in his cabin. He didn't do it quite right—the shape wasn't that of a regular shoe, but for Old-Johan it was good enough. It didn't matter if it didn't fit too well, all he wanted was something warm to put his feet into.

The thinnest leather he sewed on the sewing machine, but he quickly got angry if the machine didn't obey or if the needle broke. He'd finish the rest by hand. The stitches were not pretty or necessarily where they were supposed to be, but Old-Johan was satisfied.

"He made his shirts and underwear out of canvas. He didn't own many pieces of clothing and he wore them for a long time before he thought of washing them. When he did, he did it thoroughly. He didn't boil ashes until they became lye, as was usually done in those days. Old-Johan dumped the clothes and the ashes into the same kettle and let it all boil for a long time. Later he lay down by the lakeside and rinsed the clothes there. He never got them white—the ashes permeated the canvas, and his shirts and underwear were always dark gray.

"Old-Johan also bartered for wool when he was in Roros. He had a spinning wheel in the fishing cabin. Many's the time I've seen him busily carding and spinning. It wasn't easy to spin thin yarn by the faint light in the cabin, but he managed that too. He sat bent over the spinning wheel, treadling with a heavy foot. I was often afraid his beard would get caught in the wheel. When his homespun yarn was finished, he started to knit. He knit his own stockings and socks. Things got a little crooked when he tried to do the heels. He'd come to me for help with that, but, as soon as I finished the heel, he'd want to take over again.

"Most of the time, he wore a pair of pants he'd cut and sewn himself. He called them flappants because they had a flap in the front, which Old-Johan considered convenient and practical. He didn't like buttons on pants; he made holes with his knife, pulled his suspenders through, and fastened them with pins. If he lost a pin, he broke a new one off the nearest branch. He never built himself a privy, he did his business right out in the fields."

"I often worried about Old-Johan. I was sure he would end his days out on the lake. He was a daring fellow, and those of us who knew him best predicted that either a storm would take him or he'd fall overboard. He was not a careful man; he'd row out on the lake with his nets at the craziest times. To him, bad weather was a challenge. I have seen him return from the lake many a time, so wet and covered with slush that he practically crawled to his cabin.

"He did everything by himself, even pulling in the sweep-net. He anchored one end on land, rode out in the boat and pulled net and fish ashore, cursing or chattering happily, depending on how it was going.

"Old-Johan developed his own methods. He

obtained white flour by bartering in Roros, made a kind of clay with it, and calked the fireplace in the fishing cabin. He put out flour for the rats too. They sometimes got better rations than he allowed himself—he was cheap and mean with himself in many ways.

"One summer, he started acting very strange. He complained about a pain in his foot, but he never wanted to talk about what kind of pain it was. When I asked about his bad foot, he suddenly became close-mouthed and looked at me with fear in his eyes; he'd stiffen, and change the subject.

"I had my own idea. I knew Old-Johan was deathly afraid of snakes. He believed snakes were extremely dangerous to man and he had a feeling they were out to get him. It got so bad that he started thinking there were snakes in much of what he needed to stay alive. I tried to talk to him about the snakes a few times, but he would get sort of scared and fall silent immediately.

"During this period I took more and more notice of him. His foot got steadily worse. I could see him limping around the fishing cabin down by the lakeside. He often looked discouraged, and he changed a lot. He didn't want to eat; I tempted him with milk and bread, but he had decided to go hungry. 'I have neither head nor feet anymore,' he said jokingly, but he meant it seriously. He shook his head and looked as if he were carrying a burden he had to manage on his own.

"One evening I went to see him; I didn't have the heart to watch the lonely old fellow torture himself the way he did. When I came in, he was lying on a narrow bench in front of the stove. As usual he 'lived' in his clothes the year round, day and night, and I noticed that his pants were stiff and soiled. The pillow under his head was black from ashes.

"Old-Johan was in very bad shape. He was shivering feverishly and complained of great pain. The old man was quieter than usual and a kind of misery had come over him. There were long silences between the brief words we exchanged. There was nothing I could do except be patient. After a while he loosened up, became more relaxed, and I dared to ask: 'Could I see your bad foot, Johan?'

"He didn't answer right away. Then, in a muffled voice, full of desperation, he said: 'The snake bit me. Out in the woodshed.'

"We said no more than that to each other. I went quietly out of the cabin, determined to do what had to be done. I went straight up to Haugsetvolden and told Jo that a snake had bitten Old-Johan. He acted quickly. He threw a sack over his shoulder, took the ax out of the wood stump, and went off to the west, to the mountains and Borrfjellet. That's where some twisted, ugly old pine trees stood, with hard, old bark. Jo came back with the sack full of this bark. We boiled it in a kettle and got a strong mixture we called bark stew. I poured the stew into a pail and took it down to Old-Johan. Jo didn't say anything about coming along, he knew that I was the only one allowed in now.

"Old-Johan looked into the pail and nodded. He realized what kind of medicine I had brought and he blindly believed that only bark stew could save his foot and his life. His foot looked awful, it was as rough as a log, and many different colors.

"I washed his foot thoroughly with the strong bark stew, and when I left, I saw his face shine with gratitude through his beard. . . . After a few days, he got better, but he never mentioned the snakebite to anyone."

"In 1936, which was the last year Old-Johan was alive, he needed help and care. He wouldn't let anyone besides me come inside the door of his cabin. He wanted to continue living surrounded by the mess and the dirt he was used to. He had money in the bank in Roros and he asked me to take out an amount for him once when I was there. The amount was so small that I took it upon myself to take out an extra hundred kroner. Old-Johan was getting so weak that the money would come in handy and we only rarely went to the bank.

Anna holding the bear skull that has hung
on the pantry wall for almost a hundred years.

Winter on Haugsetvolden. In the course
of her life, Anna has had to use
the sled to bring fuel down from the mountains,
often at appalling physical cost to herself.

Anna is eighty-two years old
but she still must pull the cart herself.

Evening in the farmhouse. Anna and
Johan Haugsetvolden pray together. Johan
was the last surviving
member of the family she served.

Johan in the old stone shelter on the east side of the lake, where the farm people have always sought refuge when a storm was raging.

Anna dancing with a friend,
Vidar Sandbeck.

From the boatshed,
Anna rowing out to fish.

Anna watching over the memory of the family
she served until their death. It was she
who arranged for a gravestone to be erected
for them in the churchyard in Somadalen.

"Old-Johan did not like my having taken out more money than he had asked for. He didn't want the hundred kroner bill in the fishing cabin.

"A couple of days later, in the evening, I happened to see him struggling up the hill past Haugsetvolden. He was wearing his long coat and his strips of sackcloth around neck and legs. He disappeared between the trunks of the fir trees to the west. He had decided to go over the mountain to Rendalen, more than twenty-five miles away, to put the one hundred kroner in the bank there.

"He got no farther than Brenna, two and a half miles from Haugsetvolden. He just couldn't go on. He was so tired by then that he didn't even have the strength to go back home to the fishing cabin. He built himself a fire. First he placed two logs on the ground, then he got some kindling and put a third log on top. He spent the whole night at the foot of a big pine tree, smack up against the fire.

"When he came down from the mountain the next day, he looked shaky. He was in his stocking feet because he had taken his shoes off by the fire the night before, and they'd burned up. In the morning they were standing by the embers like pieces of black bark.

"Old-Johan wasn't going to need shoes anymore. He was ill and things were clearly going downhill. The doctor, the mayor, and the minister came to offer their help and to try to get him to leave the pigsty where he lived. He just told them to run along; he'd managed his own life until now and could manage his own death as well. He told them that if it became necessary, I would sit with him to the end. I had promised him I would.

"I stayed with him in the fishing cabin the last three days and nights of his life. He was in tremendous pain, screaming from time to time at the top of his voice and throwing himself from side to side in his bed. By this time he was very weak.

"There was a moment when he felt a little better; he looked at me quietly and said: 'Anna, please read and sing to me.'

"I realized that his mind was set on his last journey. I couldn't sing but I would read to him. I knew he wanted to hear words from the Bible. I knew he kept the New Testament in the cupboard. I found it there, and he asked me to read the words: 'For God so loved the world that he gave his only begotten son . . .'

"I could tell from the expression on his face that the words were a comfort to him. He wanted to say something but he had trouble getting it out. After a while, he was able to pull himself together. He said, in a low voice: 'I'll be going soon, Anna, never to return. I would have liked to be of some help to you, too. To thank you for the many times you have been kind to me . . .'

"Then he confided his last will and testament to me. This time he didn't forget the poor.

"Right after he'd finished, Jo Somaen, an older man from Somadalen, came down the hill from Haugsetvolden. He had heard about Old-Johan's condition and had come to sing by his bedside. Old-Johan wanted him to sing, and Jo Somaen sat in the faint light, secure in his faith, and sang 'Deep, Quiet, Strong, Mild' and 'Jesus, You Direct My Thoughts.' The waves broke gently against the boat and the net outside. It was a good moment for us all.

"Night fell. It would be the last and the worst night for Old-Johan. His pain increased; I didn't move from his side. All of a sudden he said, 'Anna, I can't stand it anymore.' He hit the side of the bed with his fist. 'You've got to get my rifle.'

"I pretended I hadn't heard what he said. I sat down on the bed and put my arm under his head. He died right afterward. 'Yes, yes' were the last words he spoke. To me it seemed that he was saying 'Yes' to death to be free of the pain.

"I laid him out nicely on the bed, closed his eyes, read 'Our Father' over him, and shut the door of the cabin. The night was still, the only sound was the gentle splashing of the lake. Old-Johan's boat was pulled up next to his net. It all seemed right."

Old-Johan was buried the day before Whitsunday. Anna and Johan went to Glotberget by boat to get the coffin. They didn't say much on the long trip back to Haugsetvolden. It was more than ten miles across the lake and they took turns rowing. They both dipped the oars in the water more quietly than usual.

On the day of the funeral, the coffin stood outside Old-Johan's fishing cabin. It was warm and sunny and the air was full of the fragrance of resin from the trees. A small group of people from Oversjodalen and Somadalen stood around together, looking serious and dressed in their finest. On top of the coffin were simple wreaths. The minister from Engerdalen spoke of the lonely man who had departed from this earthly vale of tears in the old fishing station. Then the coffin was carried down to the lake and carefully placed in the boat.

Jo and Johan Haugsetvolden rowed; Anna sat in the boat too. Several other boats followed. Lake Ister was flat and quiet with a bluish sheen and you could see the coffin with the flowers reflected in it. Anna sat looking at the western mountains. She found herself thinking that Old-Johan had been born over there, in Oversjodalen. His mother, Lavrensa, had lived in a small log cabin up the hill on Haugsetvolden. One day in early February Lavrensa went over the mountain to make sure she'd have the help of a midwife. A few days later, she came back over the mountain again on her skis with the newborn boy in a bag on her back. From the boat on Lake Ister, with Old-Johan's coffin rocking in time with the strokes of the oars, Anna had a complete view of the wilderness and the large realm of mountains where he had spent his entire life. He had felt a very strong attachment for this landscape which now was bathed in the warm June sun, waiting for a new summer. Anna thought it a beautiful setting and that Old-Johan got a fine farewell.

It was four or five miles to Somanostra by boat. From there, the coffin was taken to the cemetery in Somadalen on a horsedrawn cart. There was no church in Somadalen at the time, only a bell tower among the pine trees. Knut Nordigarden Jota rang the bells when Old-Johan's coffin was lowered into the ground.

7

Life on Haugsetvolden continued in the usual way after Old-Johan was gone. He hadn't had too much to do with either Tyri, Jo, or Johan; his world had consisted of his fishing cabin and his boat. Anna missed him. Often she looked down at the cabin by the lake and had an empty feeling about not seeing any smoke rise from the chimney and no old man moving about carrying birchwood or fishing nets.

But she had more than enough to keep her busy. Tyri and Jo were getting old; Tyri especially had

ANNA

deteriorated lately. Her back was bent like a bow now and most of the time her feet wouldn't do what she wanted them to. When she walked across the floor, wearing her skirt and apron made of different kinds of sackcloth, she pushed her left foot ahead of her and pulled the right one after. It wasn't just her body that showed the effects of the hard life she had led in the wilderness; her face had also been marked by an unkind fate. One day in the summer pasture, she had stumbled over a tree root, fallen forward, and received an ugly gash above the eye. She absolutely refused to get the help of a doctor— the wound was left to heal on its own. The rest of her life, one eyelid drooped lifelessly on her cheekbone.

From the very first day she came to Haugsetvolden, Anna realized that it was best to do as Tyri said. Tyri did not want any changes made at Haugsetvolden or any interference with the way of life there. She had her own set habits. They were not to be disturbed. Tyri's wish was the law.

February 15, 1939, was like any other winter day on Haugsetvolden. It was freezing cold, smoke rose in columns from the pipes, and the log walls cracked like gunshot. Anna was in the cow shed doing her chores. Suddenly the door was yanked open and

Johan appeared in the doorway, hatless and pale. "Anna, hurry inside, Mother is deathly ill. . . ."

"Tyri was standing in the main room, holding on to the window frame when I came in. Her body was shaking and she was pale as a ghost. She couldn't move from the spot and refused to let us touch her. She complained of terrible cramps in her foot and her back. She had so much pain that she couldn't bear anyone's hand on her. But we had to do something, so we got her into bed even though she screamed and moaned.

"The next morning she opened her one eyelid and looked at me more kindly than she usually did. 'Anna, I am paralyzed' was all she said.

"Tyri was right. From that day on, she spent her life in bed or on the edge of it. When she felt strong enough, she sat in a heap on the edge of the bed with her head to one side. I have never seen anyone quite so helpless. She had to be cared for like a baby, and when she got depressed it wasn't always easy to find a consoling word for her.

"Sometimes the smallest thing can be important. During the five years she spent in bed, the cat we kept at Haugsetvolden was a great joy to her. It lay purring in the crook of her arm and made things cozy. Her hand played in his fur for hours in a quiet, friendly way. When a stranger came near her, the cat was furious and threatened to attack. Each time this happened, we noticed a faint smile around Tyri's mouth. She didn't feel completely defenseless.

"I was with Tyri when she died. She asked me to sit by her bedside and hold her hand. All through the night not a word was said. I just sat there with her hand in mine. I remembered Old-Johan's last night in the fishing cabin eight years earlier. It was warm and summery outside then; now the cold drafts of January came through the cracks in the walls and from around the windows of the main room. She lay completely still; the clock ticked monotonously and I counted the beats each time it struck. There was a smell of burnt bark from the birch logs in the stove. I liked that smell. Through the east window I saw a couple of stars shining over Bjonnberget. In a way it seemed as though everything had stopped.

"Suddenly Tyri let go of my hand. She no longer had a grip and I understood that she didn't need to hold on to anything anymore. Her hand lay limp on the comforter, open, as if turned toward something I shouldn't disturb. Thank God, she had no death struggle—she had struggled enough in life.

"We had no way of getting a coffin. Martin Langsjoen in Somadalen helped us by building one. Until the coffin was finished, we put Tyri out in the summerhouse. I went there several times, stood next to her and found it natural to be there. One thing that happened, I have often wondered at: Tyri wasn't crooked anymore, she lay there with a completely straight back, and that is how I want to remember her.

"After we had put her in the coffin, we left it in the hall of the cow shed until the day of the funeral. It sounds strange, but we felt it was the right thing to do. For as long as she was able, Tyri's first concern had always been the animals."

Tyri was buried on February 2, 1944. It was a cold, clear winter day. The mountains around Haugsetvolden looked somewhat forbidding, just as Tyri did most of the time. The landscape had a solemn air.

"We placed the coffin inside, in the main room. A few people had come to Haugsetvolden for her funeral and to make the day as good as possible. It was wartime and food was scarce, but the guests had brought food and wreaths with them. The wreaths were made of pine branches and white paper roses. The minister of Engerdalen had been jailed in Grini, but a lay preacher came all the way from Trysil to read words from the Bible over her coffin. We sang a psalm and the coffin was carried out and placed on a sleigh.

"Johan himself held the reins and drove his

mother from the courtyard at Haugsetvolden to the grave in Somadalen. There were six horses in the procession, and the bells had been taken off them. Everyone felt that Tyri's last journey along Lake Ister should take place in silence.

"The burial in the Somadalen church was also performed by the lay preacher from Trysil. I wasn't sure it was right to do this, and that worried me. I wanted to rid myself of my bad conscience, and one Sunday in September, when I knew the minister was in Somadalen, I rowed across Lake Ister to Somanostra and walked up to the church. I told the minister everything. He just nodded at me and said that it could be left as it was. I was glad because Tyri's last journey had been just right for a worker bee like her. There was no need for a minister's robes and more psalm-singing by her grave. Peace was best for all of us now."

8

From the very first time Anna came to Haugsetvolden, she felt that Jo, who was seventy-four years old then, understood her situation and wished her well. He was considerate of her when the day's work became too hard and he often had an encouraging word. He was a stately man of the mountains, who had other interests besides hunting, fishing, and the usual work on Haugsetvolden. Anna marveled that he kept a diary of all the events at Haugsetvolden, great and small, since he had had almost no schooling. He liked sitting with a book when he had time to read.

Jo Haugsetvolden had had a difficult youth. He lived with his mother, Lavrensa, and his foster-father in a crude cabin they had put up in the fields at Haugsetvolden. When winter came, they traveled over the mountain to Rendalen, more than twenty-five miles away, but they returned to the cabin as soon as conditions were good enough for them to come back east to Lake Ister.

Sometimes Jo moved to a small island up in Hola in Oversjodalen with Lavrensa and his foster-father. They spent several winters there in an old cottage.

"Jo often told me about those days. His foster-father was a lazybones, said Jo, and many times the little boy was sent out to beg for food from farm to farm. Lavrensa made hair nets and garters, which she went around selling. In the winter she went on snowshoes to Somadalen, miles away, in order to get a little food in exchange for the things she made. Jo said that no one gave a hoot for him and his mother, and that they often went to bed so hungry that their stomachs ached.

"Worst of all was his foster-father's anger and his lack of understanding. Sometimes Lavrensa took Jo and ran away to Vedholmen in Lake Ister with him. She'd sit there all day before she dared to row back home again. Then something happened one day during coal burning that Jo could never forget or forgive. The foster-father didn't think Jo was doing a good enough job, even though the little boy did the best he could. Jo was used to beatings but that day he was beaten worse than ever before. The foster-father had cut off branches from a willow tree and tied knots in them, and Jo got a beating that burned his back and his mind for a long time.

"Jo also told me about something that had made a strong impression on him the first time he went over the mountain to Rendalen. It was in 1865, when Jo was eleven years old. A young man from Rendalen had killed his mother with prussic acid because she had refused to let him marry the girl he loved. Jo arrived in Rendalen the day of the execution. The scaffold had been raised on the spot where the evil deed was done—next to where the soccer field in Elval is today. Jo saw the scaffold. It had a bloody cloth hanging on it, to scare and warn all who passed that way.

"People had come from all over to witness the execution. Jo remembered being told that many of those who had climbed the trees around the scaffold to watch the executioner do his job had fainted and fallen to the ground. The main room at Haugsetvolden always seemed eerie to me on the evenings when Jo sat in the twilight, telling of this sad memory.

"He was often more open with me than I expected. I had never hidden anything about my life from him, so he felt it only right that I should know as much as possible about his own childhood and youth.

"One hard blow he suffered in his early years was that when he walked the long road over the mountains from Haugsetvolden to Rendalen to prepare for his confirmation, Minister Bull refused to confirm him. Jo was sixteen years old at the time. He came eight days too late, and Bull, who was in his last year as minister in Rendalen, punished the boy out of all proportion for not having come in time. Jo couldn't help it, his foster-father had kept him home to help do the daily chores in the log cabin. That day, Jo felt he had been treated unjustly and he was miserable as he walked all those miles again eastward over the mountains. The next summer he was confirmed by the minister in Engerdalen."

"I have read about Isak Sellanra in *Growth of the Soil*. To me, Jo Haugsetvolden was a man like that. First he built a small summerhouse on Haugsetvolden, where he lived with his mother, Lavrensa. They went fishing in Lake Ister a lot, Lavrensa spun linen and made nets, and Jo built a boat. He also plowed up land, built a cow shed, and acquired some cattle. In 1891 he got married to Tyri, and the hardest, most poverty-stricken wilderness living I have ever heard of began on Haugsetvolden. It is hard to believe that human beings can bear what the people at Haugsetvolden had to go through in that pitiless and roadless country.

"Jo was rather superstitious and had his own remedies for sickness. One that we often used for rheumatism was boiled anthill, preferably containing a lot of resin. Tyri, Jo, and I have all used it. We put an anthill in a large paper bag and boiled the whole thing in a kettle until we got a strong mixture. The mixture we poured into a large tub, where we soaked our feet. It had to be so hot that the steam reached the body and face. It always seemed to help. My whole body felt more limber afterward, and it was as if I could breathe more easily. On Haugsetvolden we used boiled anthill for rheumatism all year long.

"One time Jo contracted pneumonia, and I was told what I had to do. I heated coarse salt in an iron kettle and poured the salt into a bag, as hot as I could handle. I put the bag of salt on Jo's chest. I sat by his bed one whole night, and saw to it that it was kept as hot as possible. Jo really believed in anthill and hot coarse salt, but they had to be prepared right.

"The people at Haugsetvolden believed that naphtha was a good remedy, and we drank it right out of the bottle. Nobody paid much attention to toothaches—we just used to let them take their course, we were accustomed to them. On the other hand, Jo was terribly afraid of doing something that might bring down revenge. If he felt he had done someone an injustice, said or done something that could be of harm to others, he was afraid we would have to pay for it on Haugsetvolden.

"I have some of that in me too, and I take after my mother in that regard. She said to me: 'Don't ever say the word "rags" or you'll wear them all your life.'

"I have often thought of those words and of a story she used to tell: While Jesus was still walking on earth, he came upon a woman who was doing her laundry. Jesus said: 'You're washing clothes, I see.' 'I have to wash some rags,' answered the woman, who didn't own a single rag. At that instant, her wash turned into a heap of rags. Jesus walked on. He came to another woman who was also doing her laundry. Jesus said: 'You're washing clothes, I see.' 'Yes, I need some clean clothes,' answered the woman, who was very poor and had only rags to wash. The moment she answered Jesus, her wash turned into good, whole clothes."

The last years of Jo Haugsetvolden's life, he was a burden to Anna. He had hardening of the arteries and his condition was getting worse all the time. He had to be watched like a small child—he ran around aimlessly and didn't know what he was doing. She often felt sorry for him. It hurt to see a strong, powerful man of the mountains break down. There wasn't much left of the person who had sustained her for years and kept her spirits up when the prospects were bleakest. The whole management of Haugsetvolden remained in his hands nonetheless. His word was final, and that created many problems for her and Johan in their day-to-day lives.

"I recall one winter when we had neither wood nor moss on Haugsetvolden because Jo, who was eighty-five years old by then, refused to let his son Johan use the horse. We were on the verge of starvation. The only way to save man and beast was to get the loads of moss down from the mountain. Johan couldn't just let things continue in this manner, so one day he got ready to make a trip into the mountains. As soon as Jo realized what he was doing, he became furious. They were in the main room. Jo attacked Johan, hitting and kicking him. Of course, Johan was stronger than his old father. Reluctantly, he grabbed him and threw him to the floor on his back. Then he ran to the stable.

"Jo got up, his eyes rigid with anger. He was foaming at the mouth. He grabbed the rifle from where it hung from the ceiling and started for the door. Without quite knowing what I was doing, I went for Jo, grabbed the rifle, and tried to twist it out of his hands. He was too strong for me and I had to give up. He stood looking at me for a moment, his look so cold and impersonal that I thought my last hour had come. He was capable of anything. He turned away from me abruptly, staggered to the table, and hit it so hard with his fist that it split. The tabletop with the crack in it is at Haugsetvolden to this very day.

"Johan had been quick. When I hurried out to look for him, he and the horse were far to the west on their way to the moss mountain. I went to the cow shed. Now Jo could carry on all he wanted to inside. It wasn't long before the door to the cow shed was yanked wide open. There stood Jo, and I expected that it was my turn now. But he just stood there for a few seconds, all confused, and yelled in a hoarse, angry voice: 'From now on, you're on your own, Anna, I will never help you again!' With that he disappeared.

"When I returned to the main room, Jo was gone. I had no idea where he might be or what he might be up to. Could he be looking for Johan in the mountains with his rifle?

"I found Jo's footprints just outside the main house at Haugsetvolden. They pointed downhill to where he usually kept his skis upright in the snow. The skis were not there and I saw fresh tracks of skis and poles heading north in the direction of Somadalen.

"By the time Johan came back down from the mountain, it was dark. Jo was still gone, and when Johan heard what had happened, he said to me: 'You'd better go look for Father, Anna. I don't dare come along.'

"I didn't answer. I was relieved that we had got a load of moss down from the mountain and would be able to survive the next few days. I looked forward to melting down the moss and giving it to the animals. They were in pretty bad shape.

"I prepared myself for a night that was bound to be one of uncertainty and danger. I have always noticed that, at times like this, people have more courage and endurance than usual. That's how it was with me now. As I went out into the night to ski north to Somadalen, I was somehow not afraid of anything. I stopped at a couple of places, but no one had seen Jo. He could have lost his way and gone east on Lake Ister or west to the mountain. I had lost his tracks in the dark.

"I took a different way home, past the farm of Nordre Somaen. I had no sooner gone in than there was a noise behind me in the hall and Jo came stumbling in, soaked with sweat. He looked dangerous. He was still very angry and, as soon as he set eyes on me, he turned around sharply and went right back out again.

"That night I followed Jo like a fox. The old

man poled his way through the snow along Somaa and onto Lake Ister. When I saw him take the direction of Haugsetvolden, I thanked God. I was afraid he would discover that I was following him, yet I didn't dare let him get out of earshot. Everything was peaceful around us. The silence was broken only by the sounds of our skis and the gasps that came from an angry, panting Jo.

"I noticed that he was getting more and more worn out. He rested frequently, leaned on his poles and talked to himself. I could tell from his voice that he had quieted down. I walked behind him, wondering what would happen if he wasn't up to going on. What could I do if this heavy man ran out of strength?

"We got to a point north of Haugsetvolden. There Jo fell. He lay in the snow, completely exhausted. I skied up to him, but he didn't notice me right away. 'You can't stay here, Jo,' I said as forcefully as I could, while still showing my concern. 'Ask Johan to come and get me with the horse,' was his reply. He sounded resigned and almost tearful. I knew him so well that I could tell he was still angry. 'I can't leave you here, Jo,' I said. 'You'd die.'

"I took hold of him and, using all my strength, got him out of the deep snow to a standing position. He leaned against me for support, and slowly we moved forward. That's how we skied, step by step in the night, until we got to Haugsetvolden. He was soaked with snow and sweat when we got home, but he stubbornly refused to take off his clothes. The old man went to bed totally drained and as wet as if he'd gone through the ice on Lake Ister.

"He was never himself again after that trip. His body was sick too, he was more and more bothered by what we called 'the old man's sickness.' He decided that it would help if he washed with kerosene. I hid the jug, but he found it one evening while I was in the cow shed and washed his stomach and his back with kerosene. After that he lay down fully clothed in his heavy coat. The skin came off his body in great patches, and his system was poisoned. He died soon after. I think it is safe to say he died after a full life."

9

Spring and summer were on the way, and Anna was happy about that. She was tired from the long winter and the troubled time before Jo died. Thinking about sunshine and warmth made her feel stronger, and she sat for long periods by the east window and watched the approaching summer change the landscape. It was a big event for Anna, the day a wagtail bobbed up and down on the sawbuck outside the woodshed. She felt this was her thanks for all the crumbs she'd sneaked and scattered behind the summerhouse for the little birds who stayed the winter.

Anna often felt sorry for Johan. She knew he loved Haugsetvolden, but Tyri and Jo were the old-fashioned kind who held on to the reins to the end. When he finally took over and felt the weight of responsibility, he was an old man.

"Many times, without Johan knowing I was watching, I have seen him walk around and carefully examine the buildings on Haugsetvolden. They looked as if they were ready to collapse. Time, weather and the wind had worn the houses down. A log had slid out here and there, a door hung crookedly, a roof was about to collapse. It was hard on Johan, because he knew it was too late to get started on repairs. He didn't have the strength, nor could he manage the economic side of it.

"He still dreamed of fixing up Haugsetvolden to preserve it for posterity, even when he was a very old man. That's how we all feel about the things we love, we want them to survive us. I understood exactly how Johan felt the day he stood crying behind the main house. I could have done the same, because I loved Haugsetvolden too."

"Both Jo and Johan were more open with me than with other people. Many times they told me things they never mentioned to anyone else. It was a real pity that they were often so hard on each other and that Johan never got over the great fear he had of his father. Johan used to say: 'Father was often very strict.' He was thinking of the many times he didn't dare eat his fill: Johan ate in secret as soon as Jo wasn't looking, and he sat petrified with what food he'd been given. For many years I didn't dare touch the food at Haugsetvolden either, until I was certain that I was entitled to it. I was happy when I got enough not to go hungry."

"Christmas Eve on Haugsetvolden was not very special. The first time I ever decorated a Christmas tree was during the war. I wanted very much to do something out of the ordinary, we needed it so. I put on my skis, picked up the ax, and went up to Finnteltrosta, where I knew of some bushes. The decorations weren't very fancy. I used a few candles left behind by some tourists, and cut out paper which I folded into roses. We made rice porridge; we never bought anything special. But the horse and the cattle got a little extra on Christmas Eve—some oats and a pinch of flour. And Tyri walked around the cow shed and patted each animal. 'It's Christmas Eve, my cow,' she'd say.

"Jo and Johan washed and changed for Christmas Eve, but Tyri never did. She wore the same skirt as in the cow shed, weekdays and holidays. Every

ANNA

Christmas Eve, Jo sat at the head of the table and read the Christmas gospel by the light of a kerosene lamp. I liked watching him—there was something grand about him on these occasions. The Christmas scripture suited him, and in a way it didn't seem far from Bethlehem to Haugsetvolden. I could imagine Jo as Joseph in the stable; the shepherds reminded me of my own goat-herding days and we kept a flock of sheep on Haugsetvolden too.

"The moment I really looked forward to was when the church bells in Somadalen rang to welcome Christmas. That happened every Christmas Eve around five o'clock. We'd stand on top of the stairs outside, expectantly, listening for them to sound from the northwest. It wasn't Christmas until the delicate, familiar ringing reached us and then floated away over Lake Ister. If there were stars up in the sky on Christmas Eve, Jo used to interrupt the listening to say: 'There'll be plenty of cloud-berries come fall, I see. . . .'

"After the others had gone inside, I stayed behind on the stairs a little while longer by myself. I wanted to listen to the bells as long as they rang. Each Christmas Eve it was as if I was hearing the church bells of the Asmarka chapel in Ringsaker. If I saw a big star above Bjonnberg mountain, I made believe that it was also shining right then above the church of my childhood."

When Anna talks about Johan, she always mentions his right hand. It was badly hurt one winter in Somadalen. Johan was still a young boy when the accident happened. He had gone along to chop frozen moss. The ax hit his hand and made an ugly wound. Johan refused to go to a doctor for help. He handled the matter himself by sewing the wound together with needle and thread. 'See, everything is as it should be,' he said each time he told the story, and held out his stiff right hand.

"He drove himself hard when he was in the mountains and took chances. He wasn't always lucky. Late one fall he went fishing for whitefish up north in Elvalsvollen. The ice was shiny and conditions were fine, but it turned out to be a tragic day for him. His father was still alive at the time and was up on Lake Ormuttu that day, cutting *isstorr*, grass that showed above the ice. Jo would stuff the grass into cloth bags and pull them home to Haugsetvolden on a sled.

"On his way home, Jo was right above Vedholmen in Lake Ister, when he saw his son Johan moving along fast on the ice with his sleigh. Suddenly Johan disappeared, and Jo knew he must have driven into a hole. The lake is deep there, and every second counted. Old Jo didn't stop to think, he just ran down to the lake and onto the ice. Johan was struggling in the icy water and Jo saw him go under a couple of times. The ice beneath Jo was becoming unsafe. He lay down on his stomach, tore his knife out of its sheath, and chopped his way to the hole. There he got a hold of Johan's collar just as he was about to go under again. Johan was already so exhausted that he couldn't help much, but Jo, who was about eighty years old when this happened, was strong enough to get his son out of the hole, onto the ice and to land.

"The moment Johan came in the door at Haugsetvolden that day in late fall remains etched in my mind. His face was snow-white, his eyes were wet and full of fear, and his clothes were completely drenched. We placed him on his stomach in front of the stove in the main room. I knelt next to him and massaged his body. From time to time a lot of foam came out of his mouth. That meant there was hope and I knew we would be able to keep him alive. I felt thankful that evening and did not forget to thank Him who I believe had a hand in all this.

"This wasn't the only time Johan almost lost his life by drowning. One fall he and I were near Digernestjonna, on the east side of Lake Ister. We had cut reeds at the edge of the lake and had a big boatload ready for me to row to Haugsetvolden. We were not far from land, but the water suddenly deepens there. The boat gave a sudden jerk and I saw Johan fall overboard and disappear. He himself was about eighty years old at the time and didn't know how to swim. I ordered myself: 'Anna, keep cool. Get the boat closer to Johan!'

"Fortunately, I was used to handling the boat. I got it closer to land, to where Johan was thrashing bareheaded in the lake, with his hands waving in the air. I maneuvered it right next to him and he managed to grab hold of it. I inched carefully to the front of the boat to help him in. At one point it looked as if the boat would tip over and Johan would let go. He was wearing heavy clothes and hipboots, so it wasn't easy to get the old man back in. For a while I thought it was hopeless, but then I got a good grip on his jacket at the back of his neck and was able to pull him out. I admired him then; he was shaking with cold where he sat in the boat, but he was lucid and tried to keep the conversation going while I rowed west to Haugsetvolden. Later, when he told of his dip near Digernestjonna, he used to say: 'But my black fur hat I never saw again after that day.' "

"One day before Christmas the same year, Johan and I were on our way to the church in Somadalen. We walked along the river, which runs crooked in these parts, and the ice was not safe. Johan believed it was strong enough. He always carried a hatchet when he knew we were going to walk on the ice and he was carrying it now, but he felt so safe that he didn't use it.

"He should have. Near Storkroken, as the big bend in the river was called, he stepped through the ice with one foot and fell backward. He almost couldn't move and lay there helplessly.

"I didn't have anything that might be of help. Johan had the ax. This part of the river is incredibly deep, so I knew I had to move very carefully. I crawled toward him. The ice was cracking under me and I was terribly scared. The yards seemed many and long and it felt like an eternity before I reached him. I grabbed his foot and pulled him after me over the ice toward land. He complained bitterly about his foot; he had twisted his ankle badly when he stepped through the ice.

"I felt sorry for him, sitting in the snow and shivering. For the first time I saw that he had really become an old man who was dependent on others. I sat down next to him in the deep snow, took off my stockings, and gave them to him.

"Johan no longer wanted to go to church. He knew his fishing companion Peder Tollan was in the fishing cabin in Elvalsvollen. He wanted to go too. He limped over and stayed there several days.

"His leg hurt far into the winter, but he never mentioned it. On Haugsetvolden it was customary to keep aches and pains to oneself. I knew Johan so well that he couldn't hide his pain from me. My heart ached for him as I watched the old man getting ready for winter fishing east on Lake Ister. He never complained. On the contrary, he looked sort of pleased when he came up the hill from the lake with some fish.

"I have often had fun remembering the stockings I lent Johan in Storkroken. Something similar happened to me later on. Mekkel Kroka had died in Somadalen and I was on my way to his funeral. I was walking on the frozen lake and a little way above Elvalsvollen the ice burst under me and I fell in. I got back out and hurried on, soaking wet and scared. The first place I got to was Ronningen and I walked in.

"Only Jostein was home. The others had gone to the funeral. He was eight years old and I had to smile when he offered me his stockings. They were light blue. The color didn't mean a thing to me, I just wanted to get to Mekkel Kroka's funeral. He had always been very kind to me and would only have chuckled at the sight of the stockings. I accepted the eight-year-old's offer with thanks and hurried on to church. Those were surely the palest blue stockings ever seen at a funeral."

"Johan and the horse at Haugsetvolden were good friends. They worked side by side a great deal and

I always had the feeling that they trusted each other and felt safe together. That became very clear to us one winter when Johan had been to Roros and was on his way home with a heavy load. The bad weather had started, and by the time man and horse arrived at Martin Langsjoen's place it was late at night. They were still four miles from Haugsetvolden, it was below zero, and Johan sat frozen stiff and exhausted on top of the load. Martin Langsjoen tried to talk Johan into spending the night, but it was no use. Johan knew he was expected at home on Haugsetvolden.

"This is how Martin Langsjoen tells about that night: 'I poured a shot into Johan Haugsetvolden before I got him back up on the load. I heard him singing in the mountains. Johan and I both felt safe because even if he fell asleep, the horse would find the way to Haugsetvolden. He had gone that way countless times and knew where he belonged.' Blakken did not disappoint us. Back at Haugsetvolden, we were glad when we heard the tramp of the horse and the sleigh runners creaking outside the stairs in the winter night."

Johan Haugsetvolden created a lot of trouble for Anna day and night during the last three years of his life. He walked around in a daze and had to be watched like a child.

"One evening, in winter, he ran outside in nothing but his underwear and socks. I didn't get a chance to stop him and he walked several hundred yards in the deep snow before he fell. I struggled to get him back on his feet but he kept sinking deeper in the powder. I was standing in the deep drifts up to my waist and couldn't get a good grip. I got him on his feet several times but he kept keeling over again. I was afraid this would be the end. I had to leave him, get the sled, and rely on being able to get him on it.

"It worked, but after all the work of getting through the snow to the stairs, he started to struggle. He refused to go inside and fought against it with all his might. He was excited and nervous and not to be reasoned with. He just lay down in front of the door and there was nothing left for me to do but try with a rope. I managed to slip it under his back, tied a knot on his chest, and pulled him a little bit at a time to the entrance, across the doorstep and onto the floor. He quieted down there, but he was ill and worn out.

"After this, I watched over him for several weeks, sitting by his bedside day and night. I knew what was coming. Hour after hour, I dipped a rag in some water and wet his lips with it."

On the night Johan Haugsetvolden died, August 27, 1968, Anna lived through something she never

ANNA

---

talks about. It isn't like her to tell anyone, but what happened was that Johan lay in bed, waving his arms toward Anna. She understood that there was something he wanted to say and bent down over him. Johan looked pleased, he had a happy expression on his face, and the words he managed to say came out quietly: "You have always been so kind, you . . ."

These were Johan Haugsetvolden's last words. He didn't have time to thank Anna, but what he had said filled her with joy. She got up quietly and said "Our Father" over the last member of the Haugsetvolden family.

10

Anna was not yet all alone on Haugsetvolden. Jenny was still with her—she was a homeless woman, placed on Haugsetvolden by the poverty board the first year of the war. She wasn't very bright or capable. She had a difficult and dangerous disposition and no one wanted her. She was sent from place to place and became more and more a stepchild of society. Anna felt for her; she knew what it was like to be placed with strangers and to be insecure.

Obviously, she would find room for her on Haugsetvolden.

"Jenny had to be tended constantly. I had to look after her and take care of her all the time. I did it for years without receiving a penny for her. After Tyri and Jo were gone, Johan and I discussed what we ought to do about Jenny. We quickly agreed: she would remain with us as long as anyone lived at Haugsetvolden. We both pitied her and considered it our duty to give her a home. We were both fond of this unhappy woman, but her mood could change abruptly, she'd turn on us all of a sudden, for no apparent reason.

"One day when I came in from the cow shed, Tyri and Jenny were alone in the main room. I had a feeling something was wrong. There was something in the air, but no one said anything. Quick as a whip, Jenny grabbed the big, heavy water ladle and came at me with her arm lifted, screaming that she was going to hit me. She had no control over herself and her face was full of hatred and anger. I managed to avoid her and escape through the door, and I ran down to the fishing station, where I hoped to find some fishermen in the cabins. But they were out on the lake and I could think of no other way out, so I ran up the hill to Haugsetvolden and to the animals in the cow shed. Jenny, who was a big, strong woman, was running after me the whole time, threatening to knock me down.

"We got to the cow shed at the same time. We were both out of breath and each scared in our own way. I can't explain why I felt I had to be near the animals. Then a strange thing happened. As soon as we were in the cow shed and the cattle turned toward us, Jenny quieted down. She let go of the water ladle, and it dropped to the floor. She started to cry, and everything was all right."

"In the late forties, Johan decided I should have my own cabin to live in on Haugsetvolden. He tore down an old fishing cabin down by the lake and put it up again in the courtyard right outside the cow shed. The cabin was small, just one room with two bunk-benches and a stove in the middle. Before, I had slept in the main room with the others and I was very pleased with my own little cabin. Here I kept the few things I owned, and living with me I had Pisi, a big black cat. Pisi was good company, we enjoyed each other. The evenings I spent with the cat in my lap and a good fire in the stove were the coziest.

"People passing through Haugsetvolden liked to tease me for living alone in the cabin with a cat. One evening, someone said as a joke: 'Anna, I'm going to set fire to this wretched cabin of yours. It isn't a fit place to live in.'

"Jenny was also in the main room and heard what he said. She didn't understand that it was meant as a joke and none of us dreamed that it would stick in her mind.

"A couple of days later, Johan and I were working in the mountain west of Haugsetvolden. We both noticed a strong smell of burnt peat and heard someone calling. It sounded like Jenny. Every once in a while, someone passing through Haugsetvolden joked around with her in a noisy way, so we figured it was all fun and games. But the yelling continued and the smell of smoke got stronger. We became alarmed and went down the mountain to a spot where we could see Haugsetvolden below.

"It was a sad sight for me. Huge licks of flame and heavy black smoke were billowing over the rooftops of Haugsetvolden. 'It's my cabin that's burning,' I said to Johan.

"I immediately thought of Pisi—he was a living creature too. Before Johan and I were able to get to it, the cabin had burned down, cat and all. I lost everything I owned. The most valuable items were two clocks and a sewing machine. But it was Jenny who needed consolation most. She skipped around me, all confused, her hair singed from the fire. She was terribly upset when she realized what she had done. She had taken kindling from the woodbasket and poured kerosene over it. Then she had found some matches and lit the fire. She had no idea that it would end in a catastrophe. She was merely following through on a notion that had come to her a few days earlier."

Anna spent many of the happiest moments she had on Haugsetvolden down in the boathouse when the weather was nice. There she either hung the fishing nets out to dry or cleaned the fish caught during the night. She always had the company of small talk that came out of the lake as the lazy waves lapped against the boat or the stones and rocks. The peat roof and the sun-scorched brown logs in the boathouse always smelled good. The fresh fish had a good, familiar smell too, and the breezes off Lake Ister were pleasantly cool.

On such a day in August 1969, Anna and Jenny stood cleaning fish in the boathouse. They were both enjoying themselves, but Anna was a little worried. Jenny had had several bad heart attacks lately and she would start crying for no apparent reason. Death was on her mind, and she often talked of Johan. She had asked to be buried next to him in the cemetery in Somadalen.

"As we were walking up the hill from the boat

shed, Jenny had a terrible attack. She almost couldn't breathe. I got her to bed, and she calmed down and fell asleep. But it wasn't long before she was up again and went outside. I didn't pay too much attention—she'd had bad attacks before.

"Then I heard some rattling outside. I hurried out and there was Jenny, lying up in the loft of the old house. She had taken a ladder and climbed up. I could see her in the loft and I could tell that things were getting serious. I had to get her back down, and I couldn't do it by myself. I ran down to the fishing station, where I was lucky to find some fishermen, who helped me get her down.

"She was barely alive and very weak. She slid out of my arms. I lay down on the ground next to her and placed her head on my chest. We stayed like that, out in the open, for two hours. Then I realized that from then on I was to be all alone at Haugsetvolden. I didn't leave Jenny until 'Our Father' was read over her also. She would receive the same blessings as the others of Haugsetvolden.

"Deep inside of me, I now felt that it was Jenny who'd been closest to me. She had needed me most of all."

11

Anna is still at Haugsetvolden. She cannot picture herself spending a day away from all that has been with her through the years, the little things indoors and the big ones out of doors in nature itself. She feels it is all part of her. Even so, she often thinks of her birthplace, and a couple of years ago she just had to take a trip to Hedmark.

"I couldn't rest until I was certain I'd be well received back home. I had once turned my back on my place of birth to take to the road with Big Karl.

People said I had hidden away in the wilderness. I could live with that, since I had chosen to live buried on Haugsetvolden and had seen it as my duty. But I never felt that this meant I'd betrayed my home town. It had remained with me always.

"I wondered if there was still a door open for me in Ringsaker. I had no high hopes. I would see what happened."

Exactly forty-nine years had elapsed from the time Anna wandered off with Big Karl until she returned to the region of her childhood. Most things looked foreign and strange to her, and the new road that ran through the village made it difficult to find the way. But the flowers in the ditches along the fences and in the fields made her feel at home. There are few flowers in the wilderness, and Anna was reminded of how rich the soil must be in Hedmark that so many flowers could grow everywhere.

There was one thing she was especially looking for that day. She wondered if she would find a short stretch of the trail leading up to Lorta. She could see it so clearly in her mind's eye—narrow and crooked as it wound its way up the wooded mountainside. Suddenly she felt a warm sensation run through her—*there* it was! She couldn't see many yards of it, but it looked just about the same as when she and her mother had hurried over it. She even recognized a flat stone she used to step on. At that moment she felt she was completely at home again. Later she did find open doors and met friendly people. To Anna it was as if a broken circle had been made whole again. Nothing inside her was fragmented any longer. She traveled back to Haugsetvolden happy and relieved.

Now Anna is glad for each new day she gets to live on Haugsetvolden. She is grateful to those who stand by her and support her wish to stay there to the end.

"Haugsetvolden became the home I had dreamt of. This is where I have used up all I had in me and was glad to do it. Now I feel safe, and that's what I wanted. Many people believe that the wilderness and the days at Haugsetvolden get lonely for me. That isn't so. I have much to think back on, and I can still picture those I have lived with here. To me, in a way, they are still here. All the bad things are gone, and the good stands out all the more clearly, just like the light of day over Lake Ister.

"I often remember the day, about fifty years ago, when I lay on the ground by the storeroom, so desperate that I dug my fingers into the earth. The voice I heard then said the only right thing—that I should stay on Haugsetvolden because it was my duty to live and work here.

"I have never been in doubt about who spoke those words. I found the strength, and I am grateful for everything.

"God and my hands have made me happy."

AFTERWORD

Others may have gone hungry even longer than Anna, known even more abject poverty, had to make do with even less good fortune. Hardship also has its class distinctions, and the scale of misery permits a wide range of readings. But nameless hardship leaves us unaffected; no one hears the appeal of anonymous poverty. Through Anna poverty has been given a new name. Her hardship and her dreams have been discovered. Her misery has been selected to be shared. Her despair is spread out for inspection. And her most precious possession, the stubborn will to survive, is made available to the public. A hard life lived in Norway's Odemark, set against long years of indifferent obscurity and framed by the limits of endurance, suddenly becomes a focus of attention that commands our intimate involvement.

But what is it about Anna's self-portrait that involves us so compellingly? Why is her account of poverty so unexpectedly "successful"? A former vagrant who was homesick for stability, she simply tells her own story; but after reading it we know more about ourselves.

Born in penury, given away to people not much better off, cowed and exploited even as a child, always hungry: Anna's childhood reminds us that scarcity, not prosperity, is the norm. The child who feels personally responsible for her own hunger presents us with something that we, accustomed to surfeit, have forgotten: the natural acceptance of hardship as a birthright. Having enough to eat, keeping warm—things we never talk about because we consider them our unquestionable, inalienable right —are for Anna always uncertain, always urgent needs that must be supplied by daily effort and endurance. Here at least she disabuses us about the so-called joys of a simple life.

Being a vagrant offers a way out of such poverty. And although Anna only escapes into another kind of hardship, the story of her years on the road with her husband, Big Karl, initiates us—at risk of sounding cynical—into the immediate attractions of vagrancy. No ties, no responsibilities—all around the vagrant the horizon lies inviting, days and seasons awaiting his command. His poverty holds the promise of a terrible freedom: a life without "petty dictators." Not that we prisoners of work contracts, possessions, agreements will find an alternative here; but we do at least see that it is possible to get by on minimal gratification. This seems to be the lesson of the road: it is our expectation of happiness that determines how much we need to be entirely free. Never lost in a crowd, never called to account, always on the move over mountains and glaciers—perhaps Knut Hamsun was right in seeing vagabondage as one particular expression of superior consciousness. But Anna's story makes it clear that life on the road would not satisfy us indefinitely. Despite the joy of breaking free, despite the compulsion of the vagrants' roving search for their own Arcadia, the desire to settle down and the need to leave behind somewhere a trace of her existence are so pressing that Anna begins to be torn by this familiar dilemma. Wandering satisfies a great variety of needs, but there is one thing it rules out completely: assuming a useful function. And Anna believes that fulfilling a

AFTERWORD

function is the only way of justifying our existence.

Excessive freedom engenders a yearning for restriction; large-scale indecision engenders a stubborn homesickness for order. This woman's life exemplifies it: her lapidary protest against the harshness of existence is expressed less convincingly in her wanderings than in taking employment on a barren farm. Fleeing, escaping do not affirm life; only staying to fight can do that—even when the weapons are inadequate.

Anna's decision to stay on the farm does not release her from either poverty or hunger. But in a mysterious way her life becomes more bearable, through the simple discovery of what it is to be needed. A pattern comes to light here, a working model: she is willing to accept even the hardest task when she sees that others are dependent on her and her work.

Of course the model is simple, and lovers of complication may well shrink from it in horror; but only the most arrogant will dispute that the discovery of being needed for the first time can be overwhelmingly significant for a human being. Certainly after the bleakest life imaginable, Anna makes it with open gratitude. In old age she acknowledges that the function she assumed had saved her life from the vagaries of chance; this was all that counted, and it outweighed her misery.

Other demons may torment us in our modern commercial world—every one of us is liable to consider life worthless under present conditions. To this extent the example of life lived in Odemark is not so remote: Anna's attempt to hold her own in a hostile world belongs in the register of archetypal human experience. In her resistance we recognize ourselves. But at the same time we see that in extremity everything assumes a different value—feelings as much as thoughts, words no less than gestures. In her story Anna demonstrates that there are hierarchies even within poverty, and that even the starkest levels can afford joy and pleasure as well as laughter.

It is understandable, for instance, that memory becomes selective in the face of despair: Anna still remembers clearly the smallest acts of kindness she received in the distant past; she knows by heart all the dates of decisions that made life better or worse for her. She confirms that poverty endows its victims with a special instinct: outcasts recognize each other instantly, and will attempt to help each other out of difficulties. However, we shouldn't assume any basic unbreakable solidarity among the poor, and Anna's example shows that suffering is by no means a shortcut to virtue. In her laconic psychogram of poverty no one drowns in self-pity, and there is never the time to wallow in emotion.

Nevertheless, hardship enforces its requisite code of behavior. Everyone measures his own food ration; that is, everyone eats as much as he feels he has earned. No one on Haugsetvolden talks of pain except in emergencies; everyday illnesses are not mentioned, no one has ever had a toothache because it is suffered silently until nature cures it. Endless tasks are invented to fill "spare time"; the women knit furiously as they are driving the farm animals into the forest. Anna can't be choosy about the work she does just because she's a woman.

But the narrative shows that even in extremity—if it lasts long enough—human beings are capable of all the responses and feelings that a normal situation would allow. In Anna's manifesto nothing is missing from the spectrum of experience—it's just that every response is more restrained, more precisely apt. Falling through ice and wetting a stocking is the occasion for laughter. Gutting fish at the landing stage affords genuine satisfaction. And there's pleasure, pure pleasure, in hearing the sound of Christmas bells from a distant fishing village. These feelings are in no way sentimentalized. A life of such hardship calls forth its own mode of expression. No one on the barren farm is totally confiding. The listener hears just enough praise or blame to glean the impact of the statement; he must imagine the rest for himself. Hoarding words is a way of increasing their value.

Above all, this peripheral tale demonstrates convincingly that nothing is peripheral. Wherever men suffer poverty and fight hardship, wherever one of us finds a last resort to meet the challenge of existence, there is an example, a model: we confront the very center of being. Which is why after reading Anna's life story we know more about ourselves.

SIEGFRIED LENZ

PUBLISHER'S NOTE

When this book appeared in the original Norwegian in September 1972, Anna was very much alive and active. Early in 1973, however, she fell ill and spent some time at a hospital and later with a family in Osterdalen. She died on May 17, 1973, and was buried on May 23 at the Hunn Cemetery in Gjovik, in a simple ceremony where only her relatives and a few friends were present.

A NOTE ABOUT THE AUTHOR

Dagfinn Grönoset was born in Trysil, Norway, in 1920. He is an editor of *Östlendingen,* a newspaper in the Norwegian city of Elverum. A working journalist, he is also the author of many books. This is his eleventh.

A NOTE ON THE TYPE

The text of this book was set on the Linotype in Optima, a typeface designed by Hermann Zapf from 1952 to 1955 and issued in 1958. In designing Optima, Zapf created a truly new type form—a cross between the classic roman and a sans-serif face. So delicate are the stresses and balances in Optima that it rivals sans-serif faces in clarity and freshness and old-style faces in variety and interest.

This book was composed, printed, and bound by the Haddon Craftsmen, Inc., Scranton, Pennsylvania.

The map of Norway is by David Lindroth.

The book was designed by Earl Tidwell.